The Open University

A221 State, Economy and Nation in Nineteenth-Century Europe

Block 2: Economy

First published in 1996 by

The Open University
Walton Hall
Milton Keynes
United Kingdom
MK7 6AA

© 1996 The Open University
Reprinted 1997, 2000 (twice)

ISBN 0 7492 1159 8

Edited, designed and typeset by The Open University.

This book is a component of the Open University course A221 *State, Economy and Nation in Nineteenth-Century Europe*. Details of this and other
Open University courses are available from the Central Enquiry Service,
The Open University, PO Box 200, Walton Hall, Milton Keynes, MK7 6YZ,
tel.: 01908 653078.

Printed and bound in the United Kingdom by Alden Press Ltd, Oxford

1.4

16351C/A221block2i1.4

Contents

Acknowledgements

Grateful acknowledgement is made to the following sources for permission to reproduce material in this unit:

Unit 7

Figure

Figure 1: McEvedy, C. and Jones, R. (1978) *Atlas of World Population History*, Penguin Books Ltd, © Colin McEvedy and Richard Jones 1978.

Table

Table 4: Baines, D. (1991) *Emigration from Europe 1815–1930*, Macmillan Education Ltd, © Economic History Society 1991.

Unit 8

Text

Extract 1: Bairoch, P. (1969) 'Agriculture and the Industrial Revolution 1700–1914', in Cipolla, C. M. (ed.) *The Industrial Revolution 1700–1914*, Harvester Press, 1976, © Professor Paul Bairoch.

Figures

Figures 2 & 3: Tracy, M. (1982) *Agriculture in Western Europe: Challenge and Response, 1880–1980*, 2nd edn, Granada Publishing. Copyright: Landesamt für Flurbereinigung und Siedlung Baden-Württemberg; *Figure 5:* Murray, J. W. (1977) *Growth & Change in Danish Agriculture*, Hutchinson Benham, Federation of Danish Co-operative Societies.

Tables

Table 1: Bairoch, P. (1969) 'Agriculture and the Industrial Revolution 1700–1914', in Cipolla, C. M. (ed.) *The Industrial Revolution 1700–1914*, Harvester Press, 1976, © Professor Paul Bairoch; *Tables 2 & 3:* Tracy, M. (1982) *Agriculture in Western Europe: Challenge and Response, 1880–1980*, 2nd edn, Granada Publishing, copyright © 1964, 1982 by M. Tracy.

Unit 9

Figures

Figure 6: Rostow, W. W. (1978) *The World Economy: History and Prospect*, Macmillan Press Ltd, Copyright © 1978 Walt. W. Rostow; *Figures 7, 9 and 12:* Trebilcock, C. (1981) *The Industrialization of the Continental Powers*, Longman Group Ltd, © Clive Trebilcock 1981; *Figure 8:* Cameron, R. (1985) 'A new view of European industrialization' in *The Economic Review*, Series 2, vol. XXXVIII, No. 1, 1985, Basil Blackwell Ltd; *Figures 10 and 11:* Pounds, N. J. G. (1985) *An Historical Geography of Europe 1800–1914*, Cambridge University Press.

Tables

Table 2: Milward, A.S. and Saul, B. (1977) *The Development of Continental Europe 1780–1870*, Allen and Unwin Ltd, by permission of HarperCollins Publishers UK; *Table 4*: Deanne and Cole (1962) in Craft, N.F.R., *British Economic Growth during the Industrial Revolution*, Clarendon Press, 1985, reproduced by permission of Oxford University Press; *Table 8*: Portal, R. (1966) 'The industrialization of Russia', in Habakkuk and Postan, *The Cambridge Economic History of Europe VI, The Industrial Revolution and After, Part II*, Cambridge University Press.

Unit 10

Figure

Figure 13: Simon, M. (1967) 'The pattern of new British portfolio investment, 1865–1914', in *Capital Movements and Economic Development: Proceedings of a Conference Held by the International Economic Association*, Macmillan.

Tables

Tables 1, 2, 3, 4, 5, 7, 8, 9, 11, 12: Bairoch, P. (1976) *Commerce Extérieur et Développement Économique de L'Europe au XIXe Siècle*, Mouton de Gruyter, a division of Walter de Gruyter & Co; *Table 10:* Reprinted with permission of the publishers from *Economic Elements in the Pax Britannica* by Albert H. Imlah, Cambridge, Mass.: Harvard University Press, Copyright © 1958 by the President and Fellows of Harvard College.

Unit 6
Introduction

*Prepared for the course team by
Clive Emsley*

Study timetable

Weeks of study	Texts	Video	AC
1	Unit 6	Video 2	

You will also need to view TV 2 and TV 4 as you work through this block. TV 2, 'The Lyonnais: A Changing Economy', is tied directly to this block; it presents a detailed study of the process of economic development in the Lyonnais, economically the most dynamic region in France in the first half of the nineteenth century. TV 4, 'Changes in Rural Society: Piedmont and Sicily' is also relevant in as far as it addresses the different kinds of economy, and the processes of economic change, in two regions of nineteenth-century Italy.

Introduction

The introduction to Block 1 began by asking you to think about the concept of the state and its various definitions, but this is not to say that there is no controversy or complexity in studying it in the context of nineteenth-century Europe. Should we, for example, focus on *national* economies, or is it more sensible to recognize that *regions* developed at different rates and that regions are often not coterminous with state boundaries? The growth of industrialization during the nineteenth century needs to be balanced by a recognition of the continuing importance of agriculture; even as late as 1914 more Europeans lived and worked on the land than lived in towns and worked in factories (this issue is addressed directly in TV 4). Furthermore, while there was a growth of industry, there remain controversies about common patterns in this growth; and recognition of the growth of industry must include an acknowledgement of the fact that such growth was not simply confined to the products of new technology and new factories. We have selected what we consider to be four key themes in the development of the European economies during the nineteenth century and these will be addressed, respectively, in the next four units.

1   Whatever the arguments about industrialization, there is no disputing that there were many more Europeans at the end of the nineteenth century than at the beginning. Unit 7 focuses on **population,** the reasons for its growth, its relationship with other economic and social changes, and the safety valve of emigration.

2   More people meant more mouths to feed. As noted above, **agriculture** continued to play a key role in the developing economies of nineteenth-century Europe.

3   Industry in the broad sense of production for a market existed long before the nineteenth century, but during that century, in several parts of Europe, there was a generalized process of technological innovation and factory development which we encapsulate in the term **industrialization.**

4   Trade and commerce similarly existed before the nineteenth century. But how did industrialization affect **commerce,** and how did commercial activity such as banking, insurance and retailing develop? One way of understanding the 'ascendancy' of Europe, as we noted in the general introduction, is to consider its spread across the world in the shape of formal and informal imperialism. Unit 10 addresses **the development of the European international economy**.

The experience of work

Working your way through this course is, we hope, productive labour, but it is not directly adding to the national economy. How do you, or did you earn your living? What skills do you/did you require? How have they changed? Technological innovation and industrial development brought changes to the ways in which people worked in nineteenth-century Europe; let's start by thinking about work.

Video Exercise

Turn to the Video 2, Section 1, 'Work'. This section is divided into three subsections: 'The Armourer'; 'The Canuts' (the name used for the Lyon silk workers, the etymology of which is unknown); and 'The Miners'. Watch it now; note down the different kinds of work demonstrated and discussed, and the extent to which you think that they are skilled. What kind of implements do the workers need for their jobs? What kind of materials are they using, and where, do you suppose, did this originate? How far could they be supervised, and how far was the worker his own master? How far were the different kinds of work carried on in the family, in the community? How far do you consider that these kinds of work differ from (a) agricultural, and (b) factory labour?

Discussion

The video starts by looking at individuals working on their own – an armourer and a silk weaver. The work is relatively skilled: the armourer has to know how to put the gun together; the weaver is using her whole body – she sits on a narrow bench at the loom, using her hands on the shuttle and her feet on a treadle (incidentally, in the early nineteenth century, as should be apparent from the comments of John Merriman and Yves Lequin, the weaver would have been a man). The armourer uses relatively small hand tools at a work bench; the weaver requires a large, fairly sophisticated loom (in this particular instance, a Jacquard Loom developed for the Lyon silk industry at the beginning of the nineteenth century). The armourer owned his own tools; probably the early nineteenth-century weaver rented his loom. The materials used are pre-produced parts for the armourer and silk thread for the weaver, which suggests commercial networks involving middlemen handing out work to these artisans. Working at home or in a small workshop meant that the artisan or craftsman was his own master; he worked when it suited him taking an extra day's holiday at the end of the weekend – Saint Monday – if he wished. He worked with his family, using them to carry out some of the tasks associated with his trade. Lequin makes the point that miners also worked in groups based on family links. The reconstruction of the late nineteenth-, early twentieth-century mine work gives an idea of the danger of the work and perhaps too the solidarity that developed among the miners as they worked, stripped down in the heat and dark. Miners often tend to be associated with industrialization, yet the reconstruction stresses the primitive nature of the tools which they used, and their dependence on human and animal muscle power (we had to include the veteran miner Monsieur Ruiz discussing his horses!). Moreover, Lequin notes that miners were often former peasants who kept close links with the countryside (in Britain, remember, there were *pit villages*, mining communities did not live in industrial cities). Miners were rather less their own masters than the artisans who worked in the small independent workshops, yet they too did not work under the supervision of masters or employers.

Supervision is an aspect which changed with the development of the factory; workers had to clock in and clock off at set times. Ownership, or at least a proprietorial interest in the tools or equipment necessary for a job, was also something which changed with the factory. But what about agricultural labour? How far were peasants skilled as artisans were skilled?

Video Exercise   Watch Video 2, section 2, 'Agricultural Work'. How far do the seasons dictate work on the land? Where is agricultural work different from what you have just seen?

Discussion   Well, this is a very specific sort of agriculture that you see here – viticulture in the Beaujolais region of France. Agricultural work is dictated by the seasons; this film was shot at the time of the grape harvest (mid to late October) and focuses particularly on pressing the grapes. The press you see in action here dates from the nineteenth century: a series of heavy oak blocks (not unlike railway sleepers) are piled on the grapes, and then pressed down with a screw press operated by a complicated system of ropes and ratchets turned by a wheel set into the wall. This is a communal task, and the proprietor could oversee his men at this point – it was, of course, more difficult when they were working in the fields. The proprietor also provided the meals for his workers and, especially, the feast at harvest home and other key moments of the agricultural year. There were smaller presses, some of them portable moving from farm to farm. In case this is giving a somewhat idyllic picture of rural life (and perhaps the rural idyll is reinforced by Gilbert Garrier's comments on the way peasants could lend each other a hand), remember that farm work has to be done in all weathers, and that even if masters were supposed to provide for their workers, they were not necessarily generous or fair while the workers were not necessarily docile and deferential.

In English the word 'peasant' has acquired a pejorative sense; this is less the case with the French word *paysan* and the German *Baumer* but even here nineteenth-century townsmen tended to look down on rural workers. But just how primitive was agricultural work? Did the peasant lack skills? Was his life unchanging? In a very broad sense these issues are addressed in Unit 8, but for a more detailed focus turn now to the comments of Michelle Perrot and Gilbert Garrier in the Video 2, section 3 'French Peasantry'.

Video Exercise   Watch section 3 now and note down what you think might be said in response to the questions which I have just posed.

Discussion   Garrier stresses that there were a variety of different forms of agriculture in nineteenth-century France which produced a variety of peasant experiences. There were people who existed in the hard mountainous regions, and who often had to make seasonal migrations to the towns as, for example, building workers, or to other agricultural regions to bring in the harvest. In contrast, in the more specialized agricultural areas, the peasantry possessed and/or developed their *savoir faire* (know-how) in viticulture, animal breeding, grain production. However, if their skills and life styles varied, peasants appear to have been essentially inward-looking until the country began to be increasingly opened up and, in a sense, unified by the development of roads and railways from the mid-century.

Michelle Perrot calls the nineteenth century a golden age for the French peasantry, with money being brought into prosperous towns and villages, and being invested in land. This, and the artisan work with which the video began, is a far cry from what we normally associate with a period that is invariably perceived of as being increasingly dominated by the factory. Now I am not just being difficult here, nor am I trying to confuse you. The point is that there were a vast range of work experiences during the nineteenth century even within the same country. Using a discussion which I had with Michelle Perrot, I want to get you to focus now on the industrial experience of nineteenth-century France and what it meant for the people.

Video Exercise   Watch Video 2, section 4, 'Factory Work', and note down what Perrot has
     to say about an industrial revolution in France; where the workers came from (remember the peasants were keen to stay on, and invest in, the land – but France also had a demographic problem); the impact of the new factory work system on social life.

Discussion   France, she states, did not have an industrial revolution like Britain and Germany. The shortfall in the workforce was made up by bringing in a large number of foreign workers and also recruiting female labour. Understandably the bosses opposed Saint Monday, and the work regime of the factory militated against going to the café for a drink during the day. The café remained important for men, while women might find other locations for social interchange, such as the washhouse, but new sites were developed for leisure – football stadia, boxing – and so too were new styles of leisure such as reading, the cinema (at the very end of the century), and the seaside outing (obviously greatly facilitated by the development of railways).

The nature of industrialization

So far in this introduction we have addressed issues specifically relating to the work experience of individuals in the changing economies of nineteenth-century Europe, and of France in particular; we also have to explore what was happening to the European economies, and ask ourselves whether it is possible to generalize from one country's experience. To help you into such an exploration we put a series of questions to two of the leading historians of nineteenth-century European economic development, Sidney Pollard, Professor Emeritus of the University of Sheffield, and Clive Trebilcock, Fellow of Pembroke College, Cambridge. Their responses to these questions take up the second half of Video 2, 'An Understanding of Industralization'. The idea here is to get you thinking; of course, we do not expect you to acquire every nuance and detail from what is said – exploring the industrialization of Europe has, after all, been the subject of Pollard and Trebilcock's professional lives. But we do expect you to start asking yourself questions about how and why industrialization occurred, about its impact, and, if possible, to begin to question the different interpretations put before you.

Video Exercise

Already in this introduction several times you will have come across the word 'industrialization'. So, first and foremost, what is industrialization? How can we best explain it? Watch Video 2, section 5, 'Definitions' and note how Pollard and Trebilcock define it.

Discussion

Both stress the transfer of resources from agriculture to industry in the process of industrialization. Pollard emphasizes the changing type of productive unit – it becomes much bigger, requiring more capital, which provides the opportunity for capitalists to acquire a dominant role in the economy – the enlarging of markets, the freedom of labour. Trebilcock draws on four criteria developed by the American economic historian David Landes: the use of technology first, to replace human skill (and to develop new skills), and second, to replace human and animal power; the shifting of production from handicraft to factory, and that general shift from agriculture. But whereas Landes sees the process as technology led, Trebilcock favours more emphasis on institutions which developed skills and on the growth of services as well as manufacturing.

There is an interesting question which you might think about here – and it will be raised again in Unit 9 – can industrialization happen without technological change? If there were capitalists with raw materials at their command, which they were prepared to farm out to unemployed or underemployed men and women in rural communities to work up into finished goods in their homes, would this also constitute industrialization? And if not, why not?

So if we now have some working notion of what industrialization is/ was (albeit with some questions), is it possible to develop a model of the process? Well, a lot of economists and economic historians have attempted this – a model provides, after all, a kind of extended definition of industrialization incorporating a whole series of related concepts. One of the most influential of the 'model-makers' was the American W.W. Rostow whose *The Stages of Economic Growth* was first published in 1960.

Video Exercise

Watch Video 2, section 6, 'A Model of Industrialization' in which Pollard and Trebilcock discuss Rostow. What are the essential points of Rostow's theory, and what are the objections to it?

Discussion
Rostow is in the tradition of those economists and historians who have considered industrialization to be a moment of rapid change – an industrial revolution, in fact, the time span of which made it not greatly dissimilar from an event like the French Revolution. A key moment in industrialization for Rostow is the relatively short period (two or three decades) which he calls the 'take-off', when the amount of national income invested in industrial development doubles from under 5 per cent to 10 per cent or more. The 'take-off' slots into a rather longer series of stages of economic activity involving preconditions (i.e. a certain degree of wealth, favourable attitudes, skills, legal and social structures) beforehand and a drive to maturity arriving at a period of mass consumption afterwards. The basic criticisms highlighted by Pollard and Trebilcock are that the evidence suggests a much slower change than Rostow's rapid 'take-off' would suggest, and that his stages are too rigid allowing insufficient deviation from his model.

The term 'industrial revolution' has been in use since the early nineteenth century; the question is, does the term really assist our understanding of events? Was industrialization the result of a revolution, involving rapid change with a crucial period at its heart all over in a couple of decades? Or was it a much more gradual process? Modern historical opinion largely favours the latter. As for further models of industrialization, I will return to this later, but first let's consider the relationship between industrialization and economic growth. Was there economic growth before industrialization? There was. Pollard makes the point in his discussion of Rostow. What was new in the nineteenth-century variant, Pollard maintains, was that, here, there was no halt and reversal.

Video Exercise

Watch Video 2, section 7, 'Economic Growth and Industrialization'. What do you consider the key points made here? and do you agree with all of them? (Now you may feel a bit reluctant to attempt to challenge leading historians – but, as you watch Clive Trebilcock here, see if you can think of any examples of how, in the nineteenth century, it might have been possible to be a wealthy primary producer.)

Discussion
Briefly, Trebilcock argues that before industrialization countries could exploit their agriculture and trade, however subsequently there was much more of a trend towards a trade in industrial goods. It was, he suggests,

very difficult to be a wealthy primary producer. Pollard repeats his point about the difficulty of finding dates which reveal big jumps in economic growth, but argues that, during the nineteenth century, growth became more and more rapid especially as more and more sectors of the economy became involved in an industrialization process. As for my question about wealthy primary producers – might it not have been possible for a country with an efficient agriculture to have become, and stayed, wealthy by supplying its agricultural produce to those countries switching more and more to industrial processes and relying on others to feed them? In fact, this is precisely what did happen in some countries (notably Australia, Argentina, Brazil, Canada, and to some extent even the United States) which supplied primary produce to Europe, and which had developed high living standards by 1900 – this will be raised again in Unit 10.

The first country to embark on the process of industrialization during the late eighteenth and early nineteenth centuries was Britain. The question is – did it provide a model for others to follow, and if so, what exactly was the nature of that model? Rostow based his stages and his idea of a 'take-off' on his interpretation of the industrialization process in Britain. This brings us back to the general question of patterns of industrialization.

Video Exercise

Watch Video 2, section 8, 'Pioneer of Industrialization: The British Case'. What were the advantages and disadvantages for Britain in being the pioneer? What were the advantages and disadvantages for others?

Discussion

The most obvious advantage was that Britain was able to industrialize without competitors. But there were disadvantages in this: the process tended to be much longer, and the resulting problems, notably in industrial cities, consequently lasted for much longer. Every other country had competitors during its industrialization process – yet they also had a kind of package that they could take over based on the British experience, and they could be aware of gaps that might be filled by science and institutional forms.

Pollard makes the point here that every country has its own different resources (coal, iron ore etc.), different experiences and heritage, and these all feed in to the way that it industrializes.

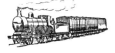

So, if all are different, is there any way that we can put an overall pattern on industrialization? Is there a model (or models) which can be used to explain the process of industrialization and which can generate rather more support than that of Rostow?

Video Exercise

In Video 2, section 9, 'Patterns of Industrialization', Pollard and Trebilcock discuss the theories of M. Hoffman and Alexander Gerschenkron, and Pollard points to some of the alternative patterns which have been (or might be) considered in analysing the process of industrialization? Briefly, what are these?

Discussion   Hoffman saw a pattern of movement from consumer goods (textiles, food processing), to producer goods (railways, engineering), to capital goods. He believed that the gap between the production of consumer goods and producer goods declined over time, and that it was possible to estimate the progress of a country from what it was producing at a particular moment. However, the boundaries between these different kinds of goods are not always clear. Gerschenkron's pattern is chronological, stressing that the early industrializers have a very different experience from later ones; his starting point is the level of 'backwardness' of the different societies. The British experience was in a society with a largely free market, economic individualism, competition among a number of small entrepreneurs, informal financial sources and little government involvement. In the mid-nineteenth century countries like France and the German states had some markets developed and some entrepreneurs, but they needed more participation from educational institutions and, particularly, more sophisticated capitalist ventures (notably investment banks). At the end of the century, when Russia, for example, embarked on its industrializing process, it was so chronically backward – with few markets, little capital, and few entrepreneurs – that it was necessary for the state to step in to substitute for gaps with managers (from its civil servants) and demand (from its military), with investment capital (from borrowing and taxation) and restructuring (e.g. with land reform).

Pollard goes on to mention the work of M. Lévy-Leboyer which suggests a very different pattern to French industrialization with a concentration on luxury goods apparently preceding the production of goods for a mass market, as found in Britain, and as would seem the logical pattern. There are further patterns which have been found in comparing large and small countries, in contrasting the dominant religion in the early industrializing countries with that of the later industrializers, and in noting the geographical movement of industrialization in as much as it began in north-western Europe and then gradually spread to the south east.

And it all seemed so simple when you began this introduction! Finally, we have touched on the way one country learned from another and we have very briefly mentioned trade, but how might these link up with the process of industrialization?

Video Exercise   Watch Video 2, section 10, 'Economic Integration and Industrialization'.
    What does Pollard see as important in the links between industrialization and trade? What kind of markets does Trebilcock describe as being formed here?

Discussion   Trade enabled a degree of technological transfer. Pollard gives the example of German entrepreneurs buying cheap British yarn and then employing low-waged weavers to undercut advanced countries (like Britain itself) or even more backward countries (such as Russia) in the production of textiles. From here it was possible to move on and progress German industrialization further. At the same time an industrially advanced country, like Britain, could provide a market for primary producers of grain or wood, and this, in turn, would enable the primary producers to boost their own resources with their own kinds of industrial development. Pollard is concerned with international trade, Trebilcock, in contrast, notes the significance of trade in developing national markets, in particular the spread of railways and the customs system (the *Zollverein*) which contributed significantly to the integration of Germany.

Think back, for a moment to Gilbert Garrier's discussion of the French peasant. The peasant was, he suggests, in many instances largely inward-looking and isolated before the middle of the nineteenth century. However, roads and railways broaden his horizons. Furthermore, as railway systems tended to be national, it is probably fair to argue that they went some way towards integrating the national communities on continental Europe and to creating national, rather than regional, markets. This is an issue which will be discussed at greater length in Block 3, but it demonstrates here, in passing, how state, economy and nation can be closely entwined.

Unit 7
Population

*Prepared for the course team by
John Golby*

Contents

Study timetable

Weeks of study	Texts	Video	AC
2	Unit 7; Documents II.1, I.2; Anderson		

Aims

The aims of this unit are to encourage you to think about:

1. the problems involved in the study of population growth in the nineteenth century;

2. Malthus's theory of population and to what extent it explains the demographic changes in the nineteenth century;

3. the reasons for the differing rates of population growth within Europe over this period;

4. the reasons for the differing rates of change in the birth and death rates within European countries during this period;

5. the extent of and the reasons for emigration out of Europe and migration within Europe;

6. the relationships between population growth and economic developments and social changes in Europe.

Acknowledgements

With grateful acknowledgement to Professor Michael Drake for his advice and for writing the footnotes to Tables 1 and 2.

Introduction

At the very start of this course Clive Emsley introduced us to the study of Europe in the nineteenth century by quoting Nipperdey who wrote, 'In the beginning was Napoleon'. He then contrasted this remark with that of Schulze who wrote, 'In the beginning was the demographic problem'. Emsley attempted to resolve the apparent paradox between the two statements by suggesting that, in their own ways, both Nipperdey and Schulze were right. Demographic changes and the changes brought about by Napoleon were both occurring at the same time and Nipperdey and Schulze were merely approaching their studies of the nineteenth century from different starting points. In many ways this is a fair and prudent judgement but I would go further and state that the two are inextricably linked. Napoleon stood at the head of a country whose population was over 27 million – the largest in Europe. He was the ruler of a unitary state whose massive manpower he could draw upon at a time when warfare was based on men on the ground. His success, in part at least, was due to this central demographic fact. If Napoleon had lived one hundred years later his chances of success would have been virtually zero given the quite massive relative decline of the French population compared with the other major powers of Europe. Once again, demographic factors must come into consideration.

The demographic problem referred to by Schulze was that of a European population which around the middle of the eighteenth century had started to increase at a rapid and alarming rate. Between 1750 and 1800 the increase was in the region of 40 per cent and between 1800 and 1900 the population of Europe more than doubled. Compare this with an estimated three per cent increase in population between 1650 and 1750.

A Europe which contained some 185 million people in 1800 was populated by 401 million one hundred years later. This increase did not take place at the same rate throughout Europe or get underway at the same time, nevertheless its effects were felt from remote communities in Finland to the growing town of Milan and from the crowded capital of Moscow to the agricultural villages of Shropshire. All classes, whether living in town or country, were affected. The rapid population growth had consequences which affected the social, political and economic life of every European country. It was associated with the break up of the old agrarian societies which had existed for centuries in most parts of Europe; it brought about an increasing movement of peoples, either migrating within or out of their own countries; and it brought changes to family structures and customs. Not only were there more people but they lived longer. In 1800 the average life expectancy in France was 28 years, by 1900 it was almost 50. The physical appearance of Europeans also altered. Seventy-two per cent of army conscripts in the period 1792–9 from one canton on the Ligurian coast were under 5ft 2in (1.50 metres) tall (Hobsbawm, 1962, p.24), whereas by 1900 the average height of a male western European was around 5ft 6in (1.65 metres).

While historians may argue whether there were Napoleonic, industrial or bureaucratic revolutions in particular countries in the nineteenth century, there is very little room for disagreement that from 1750 Europe experienced a demographic revolution.

To return very briefly to the relative merits of the 'In the beginning was the demographic problem' or 'In the beginning was Napoleon' approaches, one may well argue that the interests of the majority of members of this course team are more inclined to the latter approach. Hence a unit on population in Block 2 of the course rather than at the beginning. But if this is unfair to my colleagues, there is no doubt that the author of the set book for this course agrees with them. Only five pages of Anderson's book (376 pages in all) are devoted to the question of population. To be fair to M.S. Anderson, although his references to demographic changes are few, his account is lucid and concise and so it makes a good starting point for our study of population changes.

Exercise   Read now pp.121–4 of your set book and jot down what you think are the major points made by Anderson.

Specimen Answers   1   Unprecedented population growth (note that France is the exception in this respect).

2   The growth of population is accounted for by:
     (a)   high birth rates which reached their peaks between the 1860s and 1870s. (This is a questionable conclusion which we will discuss in the section on birth rates in the nineteenth century.);
     (b)   an even more significant factor, a fall in death rates, especially during the second half of the century.

3   While giving no reasons for the increase in birth rates, Anderson cites improved hygiene and better nutrition as being major factors in accounting for the fall in death rates, especially among young children. Nevertheless, as with birth rate figures, death rate figures varied markedly from country to country and between different social classes.

4   Population growth was sustained despite large numbers emigrating from Europe, especially towards the end of the century.

5   Population growth and the migration of Europeans to various parts of the world strengthened 'Europe's world position and influence'.

6   As a result of these changes, by the end of the century the economically active section of the population of Europe constituted an unusually large proportion of the whole, which in turn was favourable to economic growth and a rise in living standards.

Problems of sources in the study of population

Before we examine in more detail the points raised by Anderson, it is necessary to point out that the availability of statistical data, so necessary for estimating population growth, fertility and mortality rates and migration, varies widely from country to country and is particularly scarce in some countries, especially for the early part of the period. For example, while there was a nationwide census in Sweden and Finland in 1749, and Denmark and Norway in 1769, the first national censuses in England, Scotland and Wales and France were not undertaken until 1801. The first pan-German census was held in 1853, Spain held a census in 1857, and Italy had its first census immediately after unification in 1861. The first regular census system was introduced in Austria and Hungary in 1869 with the establishment of the Dual Monarchy, but the first (and only) census of the Tsar's Russian Empire did not take place until 1897. Of course, census returns are not the only statistical sources available: tax enumerations, parish registers and civil registration figures for births, deaths and marriages are available in some countries so that birth and death rates for most of the Scandinavian countries are available from the early eighteenth century. But whereas the civil registration of births, marriages and deaths started in France in 1792, a similar system was not introduced into England and Wales until 1837 and Scotland had to wait until 1856.

So, in an area of research which relies heavily on statistical data, much of the necessary data is either missing, fragmented, or untrustworthy. European demographers, of which the Cambridge Group for the History of Population and Social Structure is a prominent example (see Wrigley and Schofield, 1981), have made enormous advances in devising techniques to make use of what little data is available, in order to produce overall figures for population growth and fertility and mortality rates in England from 1541 onwards. Similar research is being undertaken in France. But, overall, it is important to remember that there is a shortage, both in quality and quantity, of data particularly for the first half of the century, and that some of the figures and evidence that I shall be using will not be as reliable a those for the end of the century.

Malthus and his ideas on population

If present-day demographers have a problem, consider how difficult it must have been for those intelligent observers living in 1800, who had little statistical material available to them to make informed judgements about the extent or the rate of population growth. What they did know was that populations were growing but, for the most part, they could only guess at what rate. What they also sensed was that this population increase was having serious consequences for the social and economic fabric of their countries. Indeed, by 1800 some observers in Britain and France believed that their countries had already reached a state whereby they were over-populated.

Right at the start of our period the subject of population growth was receiving considerable attention. By far the most famous and most often quoted writings on the subject are those of Thomas Malthus (1766–1834) whose *Essay of Population*, was first published in 1798. It is important to remember that Malthus was writing against a background of famine and war (there were serious food crises in Britain in 1795–6 and 1799–1801) as well as population increase. But he was by no means the only writer concerned with demographic problems in this period. The full title of his first essay in 1798 was, *An essay on the principle of population as it affects the future improvement of society with remarks on the speculations of Mr Godwin, M. Condorcet and other writers*. Some writers drew some conclusions similar to those put forward by Malthus. Indeed, Marx was later to dub Malthus 'the great plagiarist', which was a slightly unfair verdict, for Malthus did acknowledge the contribution made by writers, such as Adam Smith (1723–90), in formulating his ideas.

Exercise   I want you to read Document II.1, which is a few short extracts from Malthus's *Essay on Population*, and ask yourself the following questions.

1   What does Malthus see as a major factor in impeding the progress of mankind towards happiness?

2   What reasons does he give for this?

3   In what ways is this problem resolved?

Specimen Answers   1   'The tendency in all animated life to increase beyond the nourishment prepared for it.'

2   Population growth, if left unchecked, will increase in a geometrical ratio (1,2,4,8,16) while food supply only increases in an arithmetical ratio (1,2,3,4,5).

3   Malthus argues that population increases are eventually prevented by 'positive' and 'preventive' checks. The operation of positive checks on population works as follows. As population increases faster than food supply, so food prices will rise and the wages of a day's labour will purchase less provisions. Eventually this fall in food consumption will lead to malnutrition, other diseases, plagues or even famine. This will bring about a rise in mortality rates of such a size that the result will be a reduction in the rate, or even a fall in population. This will then lead to a fall in food prices, the wages of a day's labour will buy more food, conditions will improve and the mortality rate will drop. But this will lead to an increase in population, and so the cycle goes round yet again.

Preventive checks operate in the same conditions of rising population and a consequent lessening of the food supply to individuals. In these depressed conditions people will be hesitant to marry or will marry later, this reduces the rate of fertility and so there will be a reduction in the rate of growth of the population. These preventive checks, which involve moral restraint, can operate at the same time as positive checks and are distinct to man.

You may perhaps have noticed that the extract you have just read comes from the fourth edition of Malthus's essay, published in 1807. This was a deliberate choice because Malthus made substantial and important revisions after the first edition. In the first edition he set out his theory as a set of self-evident principles or laws, whereas in the 1807 edition he referred not to laws but to a model which was built up from facts and observations. One reason for this change is that during his travels on the continent of Europe he was impressed by the number of preventive checks that existed in some societies. For example, while travelling in Norway he observed that some ministers refused to perform marriage ceremonies for couples who were unable to support a family and he noticed that the absence of housing and work among some of the peasantry meant that marriage was being delayed. So by the 1807 edition, Malthus had come to the conclusion that a delay in marriage was the most powerful of the checks.

During the course of this unit we will see how relevant Malthus's ideas are to the population history of Europe; to what extent his predictions are correct and what factors occur in the nineteenth century which Malthus had not been able to take into account.

The extent of population growth

Exercise   Look at Table 1 (below), and answer the following questions.

1   What countries are growing fastest in the period 1800–51?

2   What countries are growing fastest in the period 1851–1900?

Specimen Answers   1   The population of England and Wales doubles in this period. The populations of Scotland and Finland almost double while the numbers in Norway and Sweden increase by around 50 per cent. Ireland's population increases very rapidly between 1821 and 1841 but then drops absolutely in the next decade. France, the country with the largest population in 1801, grows at a relatively slow rate compared with the other countries in western Europe.

2   Again, England and Wales have an extremely fast rate of increase, closely followed by Germany. Growth rates in Scandinavia and the Low Countries are high but the increases in Spain and Portugal are fairly sluggish. What is noticeable is that the population of France increases at an even slower rate, with an annual growth rate of around 0.1 per cent. Ireland's population decline carries on right through to the end of the century. The most dramatic increases, however, are those of the countries in eastern Europe, especially those in Serbia and Russia. Indeed, the increases may well have been even more spectacular. Remember, the first census in Russia was not

Table 1: The Population of European Countries 1801–1901 (in thousands)
(By census)

	1801	1811	1821	1831	1841	1851	1861	1871	1881	1891	1901	
Belgium				4,090		4,337[1]	4,530[2]	4,828	5,520	6,091	6,694	1=1846 2=1856
Denmark				1,231[1]	1,289	1,415	1,608	1,785	1,969	2,172	2,450	1=1834
Finland	833	863	1,178	1,372	1,446	1,637	1,747	1,769	2,061	2,380	2,656	
France	27,349	29,107[1]	30,462	32,569	34,230	35,783	37,386	36,103[2]	37,406	38,133	38,451	1=1806 2= Alsace & Lorraine incorporated to Germany
Germany			22,377[1]	26,646[2]	30,382	33,413	35,567	41,059	45,239	49,428	56,367	1=1816 2=1828
Ireland			6,802	7,767	8,175	6,552	5,799	5,412	5,175	4,705	4,459	
Luxembourg					170[1]	193	203[2]	198	210	211	236	1=1839 2=1864
Netherlands				2,613[1]	2,861	3,057	3,309	3,580	4,013	4,511	5,104	1=1829 and then every 10 years
Norway	883		885[1]	1051	1,195	1,328	1,490	1,702	1,819	2,001	2,240	1=1815 and then every 10 years until 1875
Portugal	2,932		3,026	3,061[1]	3,397	3,844[2]	4,035	4,188[3]	4,551[4]	5,060	5,423	1=1835 2=1854 3=1864 4=1878
Serbia				678[1]	830	957	1,109[2]	1,354[3]	1,902[4]	2,162	2,494	1=1834 2=1863 3=1874 4=1884
Spain							15,645		16,622[1]	17,550[2]	18,594	1=1877 2=1887
Sweden	2,347	2,396	2,585	2,888	3,139	3,471	3,860	4,169	4,566	4,785	5,137	
Switzerland					2,190[1]	2,393	2,507	2,669	2,846	2,932[2]	3,315	1=1837 2=1888
England and Wales	8,893	10,164	12,000	13,897	15,914	17,928	20,066	22,712	25,974	29,000	32,528	
Scotland	1,608	1,806	2,092	2,364	2,620	2,889	3,062	3,360	3,736	4,026	4,472	
Hungary	8,500[1]					13,192	14,349[2]	15,512[3]	15,739	17,578	19,255	1=1789 2=1857 3=1869
Austria		13,381[1]	13,964	15,588	16,525	17,535	18,225[2]	20,218[3]	22,144	23,708	25,922	1=1818 2=1857 3=1869
Russia						68,500			97,000		126,367[1]	1=1897

Italy[1]											1=before 1861 estimated on censuses which constituted Italy in 1861 2=c1816 3=c1825 4=1838
17,237	18,381[2]	19,727[3]	21,212	21,975[4]	24,351	25,017	26,801	28,460		32,475	

Source: Mitchell, 1992

Footnote to Table 1

Two important features of this table are only made clear (and then not entirely) by reference to the footnotes. The first is that the dates at the head of the table (1801, 1811, 1821 etc.) are only a rough indication of times at which population counts given below were made. Secondly, the boundaries of the countries varied over time. Thus, 'Germany' or 'Italy' in 1831, say, was not the same entity, politically speaking, as in 1901.

Because of the above it is better to calculate annual growth rates for the years between censuses. Given a pocket calculator with the appropriate keys this is easy to do by means of the formula

$$\left(\sqrt[t]{\frac{p2}{p1}} - 1 \right) \times 100$$

Here t = the number of years between p (the date of the first population count) and p (the date of the first population count) and p (the date of the second count).

Here is an example: the annual percentage growth of population of France between 1831 and 1851 is:

t = 1851 – 1831 = 20 years

p2 = population in 1851 is 35,873,000

p1 = population in 1831 is 32,569,000

$$\left(\sqrt[t]{\frac{p2}{p1}} - 1 \right) \times 100$$

$$\left(\sqrt[20]{\frac{35,873,000}{32,569,000}} - 1 \right) \times 100$$

$$\left(\sqrt[20]{1.10144616} - 1 \right) \times 100$$

$$(1.004842889 - 1) \times 100$$

0.48 per cent per annum.

To see if you have got the idea work out the annual percentage growth of population in Germany between 1828 and 1851. Here is my answer.

t = 1851 – 1828 = 23 years

p = 33,413,000

p = 26,646,000

$$\left(\sqrt[23]{\frac{33,413,000}{26,646,000}} - 1 \right) \times 100$$

$$\left(\sqrt[23]{1.253959318} - 1 \right) \times 100$$

$$(1.009887957 - 1) \times 100$$

0.99 per cent per annum.

taken until 1897 and previous totals are, therefore, only estimates and likely to be underestimates.

To sum up: at the start of the century the rate of population increase was fastest in western Europe (France being the exception), but by the end of the century it is in eastern Europe where the fastest rates of growth are seen. During the century as a whole, the population of England and Wales tripled (Scotland almost). In the Low Countries, Scandinavia and Germany, populations more that doubled over the same period. However, France, with the largest population in 1800 had by 1900 been overtaken by its neighbour Germany and almost equalled by England, Scotland and Wales. By the end of the century there were, to the east of Germany, extremely high rates of increase in the rates of population growth in Russia, the Austro-Hungarian Empire and parts of the Balkans.

(Those of you who go onto the third level course A318 *War, Peace and Social Change, 1900–1955*, will appreciate just how important these

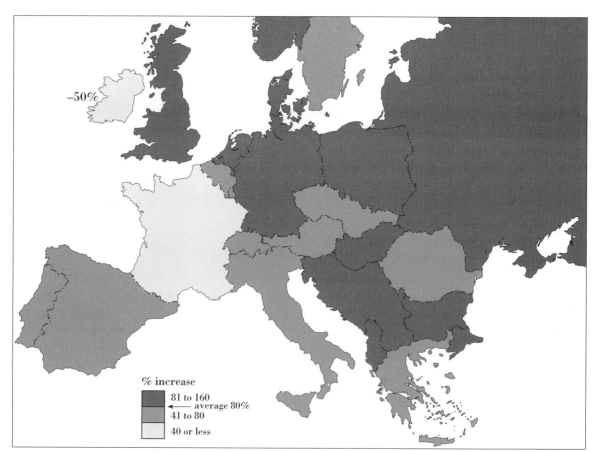

Figure 1 *Europe, percentage changes in population 1845–1914. (From C. McEvedy and R. Jones,* Atlas of World Population History, *Allen Lane, 1978.)*

demographic changes in central and eastern Europe are when discussing the origins of the First World War.)

This survey of population figures leaves us with a number of intriguing questions which will be explored in the next three sections:

1   Why was there such a rapid increase in population during this century?

2   Why was the rate of growth so uneven in Europe?

3   Why was France so out of line with the rest of Europe?

4   How do we account for Ireland's continuing population decline from 1851 onwards?

Birth rates in the nineteenth century

In his brief survey of population changes in the nineteenth century Anderson refers to an increase in birth rates reaching their peak in the 1860s and 1870s. This, as we shall see, is a misleading statement. In addition Anderson (p.122) gives no reason for the increase other than by stating that 'families were still by present-day standards very large'.

Perhaps Anderson's vagueness on this topic is understandable. Fertility rates varied widely throughout the century from country to country and, because of the relative lack of statistical evidence, it is extremely difficult to be positive about trends and rates for the early part of our period.

If you look at Table 2 you will notice, contrary to Anderson's remarks, that the birth rate in France was falling from the start of the century. The same is true for many of the German states. However, during the first three decades of the century, the birth rate in Sweden increased. Indeed, there was something of a baby boom in that country in the 1820s. There were also short-term increases after 1815 in the other Scandinavian countries. But after the 1820s the birth rates in virtually all the European countries fall. There is then a slight recovery during the middle years of the century. (This is probably what Anderson means when he states that they reached their peak in the 1860s and 1870s.) From then on there is a steady decline (although it can be discerned slightly later in some of the eastern European countries), which continues until well into the twentieth century.

Wrigley and Schofield (1981), in their massive and detailed reconstruction of the population of England in the period 1541 to 1871, reveal that there was an increase in the birth rate in the country as a whole in the late eighteenth century and early years of the nineteenth century. They argue convincingly that the principal determinant for this increase was not an increase in fecundity (i.e. an increase in fertility due to better health or diet), but a fall in the age of marriage (thereby a longer period of time for women to bear children within marriage), plus a reduction in the proportion of the population who remained unmarried. In a reconstruction of a number of English parishes, they concluded that the mean age of marriage for women fell between 1700–49 and 1800–49 from 26.2 to 23.4 years,

Table 2: Birth Rates in Europe 1801–99 : Per 1,000 Population

	1801–5	1811–5	1821–5	1831–5	1841–5	1851–5	1861–5	1871–5	1881–5	1891–5	1896–99
Norway	27.2	27.1	33.7	31.2	30.4	32.3	31.9	30.3	30.9	30.1	30.1
Sweden	31.3	32.9	35.8	32.4	31.3	31.8	33.2	30.7	29.4	27.5	26.9
France	32.3	31.7	31.4	29.6	28.1	26.1	26.7	25.5	24.7	22.3	22.1
Germany			39.4	36.0	36.6	34.6	36.8	38.9	37.0	36.3	36.1
Austria			40.0	38.1	39.6	36.5	38.9	39.3	38.2	37.3	36.9
Belgium				33.0	32.5	29.0	31.5	32.6	31.1	29.2	28.9
Denmark	32.3	30.8	32.2	30.7	30.1	31.9	30.9	30.8	32.6	30.4	30.0
Finland	38.4	37.0	38.7	34.2	35.5	36.3	36.9	37.0	35.5	32.0	33.2
England & Wales					32.4	34.0	35.1	35.0	33.5	30.5	29.4
Bulgaria									37.0	37.4	41.0
Hungary							41.7	42.8	44.6	41.9	39.6
Ireland								27.2	23.9	22.9	23.4
Romania							33.0	34.2	41.8	41.0	40.6
Russia							50.7	51.2	50.6	48.9	49.8
Serbia							43.1	42.4	46.3	43.3	39.6
Spain							38.6		36.4	35.3	34.4
Switzerland								30.2	28.6	27.7	28.5
Scotland							35.5	35.0	33.3	30.5	30.1

Source: Mitchell, 1992

Footnote to Table 2

The rates given here are so-called 'crude birth rates'. They have two advantages. First they are easy to understand, being the total number of births per year per 1000 of a given population. Secondly, they are easy to calculate if one has the number of births and a population total (usually from a census) or estimate (as, say, for a year between censuses). Unfortunately, as the adjective crude implies, the crude birth (and for that matter, death or marriage) rate can be an unsatisfactory measure of a population's fertility. For example, the crude birth rate reflects the sex distribution of a population (the fewer women than men, then, other things being equal, the lower the population's fertility); the age composition of the population (the smaller the population in the fertile age group – say 15 to 45 years – then, other things being equal, the lower the population's fertility); and the marital structure of the population (the smaller the proportion of people married – at least prior to the last twenty years – the lower the population's fertility).

One should also note that civil registration systems began in most European countries only in the course of the nineteenth century. In their early years they were not especially efficient. One effect of increasing efficiency would be an apparent, though not real, rise in birth, death and marriage rates as more and more of these demographic events were caught by the official statistics.

while that of men over the same period of time, fell from 27.5 to 25.3 years. At the same time the percentage of those people remaining unmarried fell from 15 to 7 per cent (pp.255, 265).

For all its imperfections and slimness of statistical data, no other studies involving English parishes have shown noticeably different trends from those reached by Wrigley and Schofield (Tranter, 1985, p.51).

Unfortunately, the lack of data in Scotland (see Flinn, 1977) has made similar reconstructions almost impossible. But for England, and possibly Ireland, it seems safe to conclude that a fall in three years in the age of marriage, goes a long way towards explaining the rise in the birth rate.

One explanation of why people were marrying earlier is put forward by Wrigley and Schofield in what could be called a 'delayed response' thesis. They contend that the reasons for earlier marriages were originally linked to improved economic conditions in the second quarter of the eighteenth century. Children born in this period of comparative affluence tended, when they were of marriageable age in the third quarter of the century, to marry earlier. This resulted in a growth in the birth rate in the last quarter of the eighteenth century.

Birth rates in England did begin to decline around 1815 and they then followed the pattern for most of the rest of Europe. That is, they continued to decline until about mid-century when they again rose slightly until the middle of the 1860s. Again, Wrigley and Schofield use their 'delayed response' thesis to explain the change. The 1770s and 1780s witnessed a stabilization of real wages which led to young people brought up in this period marrying later and this resulted in declining fertility rates from around 1815 onwards. However, improved real wages in the early years of the nineteenth century were followed by earlier marriages from the mid-1830s and consequently, increased birth rates from the mid-1840s onwards.

Fridlizius (1979) gives an alternative explanation for the increase in the Swedish birth rate in mid-century. The baby boom of the 1820s created a surge in the number of people in the fertile age groups in the 1850s, which led to an automatic rise in the crude birth rate. (This is what is known as an *endogenous* reason for population increase, whereas Wrigley and Schofield's explanation based on real wages is known as an *exogenous* reason.) Other reasons for the increases in other parts of Europe, especially western Europe, during these years, relate to improved agricultural production, better and quicker methods of transport and growth of industrialization, which was providing more work opportunities. In addition, migrants coming into the towns to find work were marrying earlier.

This increase, however, was comparatively short-lived and the last two to three decades of the century witnessed the start of a period of continuous decline in fertility rates. In Britain this decline started in the 1870s, Germany in the 1880s and by the end of the century, apart from Russia and Bulgaria the overall trend in the birth rate was downwards. Even in Russia the very high birth rate had fallen from over 50 per thousand in the 1860s and 1870s. Compare this (Table 2) with the birth rate in France and Ireland which was in the low 20s.

Again, we must bear in mind that this fall was not necessarily uniform throughout individual countries. For example, there was a much sharper fall in fertility rates in northern Italy than in the south of the country. In Denmark, the decline in fertility started as an urban phenomenon.

In Scotland in 1900, the live births per thousand in Lanark were 35.2, whereas in Bute the rate was 20.2 (Flinn, 1977, pp.338–9).

By 1900 the number of children born to a family in England and Wales had fallen on average to four (compared with six in the period 1860–70) while in Germany the figure was five and in France three. These figures obscure differences between different socio-occupational groupings.

Nevertheless, there were significant decreases in family sizes amongst all family groupings. In England and Wales the mean number of children born to the wives of barristers fell from 4.48 to 2.50 between 1861–71 and 1881–91 while, in the same period, those born to the wives of dock labourers fell from 7.52 to 5.67 (Banks, 1981, pp.99, 106). In Germany, in the early years of the twentieth century, while 'there were 188 legitimate births for every thousand military, bureaucratic and professional families' there were '308 for every thousand agricultural families, and 315 for every thousand families of miners' (Gildea, 1987, p.280).

The reasons for this decline are still a question of debate among historians. In England and Wales there was an increase in the age of marriage between 1871 and 1901, but the chief reason for the fall was a decline in the level of fertility within marriage and it is this factor which appears to be the predominant one in most other European countries. It appears that people in most countries, and from different classes and cultures, started making conscious decisions to reduce the size of their families and used various methods of birth control, the most widespread of which was coitus interruptus, or an increasing use of abortifacients. Sexual abstinence is another factor which must be taken into account and high percentages of the populations in European countries remained unmarried. For example, by 1911 in Ireland, 27.3 per cent of males aged 45–54 and 24.9 per cent of females, were unmarried (Finnegan and Drake, 1994, p.80).

Just why this revolutionary change in attitude occurred at this time is hard to unravel. As in most things, there is no one neat answer. The two most convincing arguments which have been put forward are:

1   As people became more prosperous towards the end of the century and as retail and consumer markets expanded, so they were faced with a choice of a large family or improving still further their standard of living.

2   In the early years of the nineteenth century in pre- and early industrial communities, children were an important factor in the family economy, where they played a part in contributing to the family income and, as they grew up, providing for the elderly members of the family. With the growth of industrialization came changes. Much industrial legislation directed towards restricting the employment of children, together with the demands of schooling, made children an expense rather than an economic investment.

One might conclude from this that decreasing birth rates are most marked in the industrialized and urbanized countries and less marked in the still primarily agrarian countries. But this generalization is too simplistic. Birth rates fell in primarily agricultural countries as well as rapidly industrializing ones. In France, where even at the end of the century well over 40 per cent of the population were involved in agriculture, the birth rate was much lower than in all other European countries.

The problem of France

As we have seen, in many ways fertility rates in France were out of kilter with the rest of Europe for most of the nineteenth century. It is true that they fit in with the European pattern of a decline in the first half of the century, a steadying of the rate between the 1850s and the 1870s followed by decline well into the twentieth century, but the level of the fertility rate in France remained much lower than the rest of the continent. For example, the birth rate in France was 32.5 per thousand in 1790, 28.1 in 1841 and 19.9 in the early years of the twentieth century, whereas the rate in Germany for the same years was, 40.0, 36.6 and 31.7.

This deliberate restriction of fertility within marriage started around the end of the eighteenth century in France. But, whereas in the cases of Britain and Germany, later in the century, the control of fertility can first be discerned among the upper classes, in France this trend can first be seen among the rural peasantry. The desire for smaller families was partly a response to French law, which stated that all heirs had equal rights to property. Rather than seeing their small-holdings continually being split up and reduced in size, many small landowners attempted, after the birth of the first son, to ensure that there was no further parcelling up of the land by practising birth control. In towns too, especially among small family businesses, there was a similar attempt to restrict family size.

However, as with nearly all demographic studies, it is important to stress that within these generalizations there are wide variations of behaviour. Some regions such as Aquitaine, the Garonne Valley and Normandy had extremely low fertility rates even at the very start of the nineteenth century, while those in Brittany, Nord and Alsace were much higher. In the department of Calvados in Normandy, in the early years of the century, the birth rate was a mere 21.4 per thousand, a level which was below average for the country as a whole at the end of the century. There were also wide variations in fertility rates between purely rural areas and, even in a relatively small geographical area such as the Department of Loir-et-Cher there were marked differences. In the rural areas of Perche, Beauce and Sologne, the birth rate was low, while in the small towns it was relatively high.

The French system of land-holding goes some way to explaining the low birth rate and the use of birth control so early in the century. The difference in fertility levels within marriage, seem so extreme compared with the rest of Europe that at least one demographer regards the extremely low birth in France as 'one of the mysteries of demographic history' (van der Walle, 1979). However, there is some evidence of birth control being used in the early part of the century in parts of Germany and Fridlizius (1979, p.345) argues that in Sweden the links between annual harvests and marital fertility among freehold peasants is 'evidence of a planned birth control'.

Conclusions

In one sense, France can be seen as leading the way in making conscious decisions regarding limiting the size of families, a trend which, as we have seen, was adopted in the rest of Europe towards the end of the century. But regardless of variations in fertility rates within Europe, what is noticeable is that, compared with most other civilizations, Europe, west of a line from St Petersberg to Trieste, had a markedly different, and perhaps unique, marriage pattern (Hajnal, 1965). The relatively late age of marriage and the high percentage of men and women remaining single, was evidence that in Europe fertility was socially, not biologically, determined. The mean ages for men at marriage has been estimated in rural areas in Western Europe at between 27 and 28 while for women it was 25 to 26 (Michael Anderson, 1980, p.18 – not to be confused with M.S. Anderson). In Norway the mean age of marriage in the 1850s was 29 for men and 27 for women (Drake, 1972, p.186). In parts of upper Bavaria, it was even higher. For example on the estate at Thalhausen in the decade 1840–9 the average age of brides was 32, while for grooms it was 33 (Lee, 1981, p.94). Once again, however, it is important to stress that there were often marked variations within regions of the same country. For example, within northern Norway, the median age at marriage of bachelors marrying spinsters in the deanery of Helgeland was 28.5 and that of their brides 26.6. In Vest-Finnmark deanery the corresponding ages were 25.1 and 23.4 (Drake, 1969, p.204).

In most other civilizations, delaying marriage until the mid-20s, was, and is, unheard of. In the great Indian and Chinese civilizations, for example, marriage was encouraged at the earliest age possible and a commentator at the turn of the twentieth century wrote of the attitude of the Turks to women as they 'repute them old women, or past the age of love, who are come to the age of 25' (cited in Macfarlane, 1986, p.216). Most contemporary developing areas in Africa and Asia have a markedly lower average age of marriage.

Exercise   Earlier in the unit I stated that we would examine how relevant Malthus's ideas were to the demographic changes that took place in this period. So, from what you now know of the changes and fluctuations in birth rates in the nineteenth century, jot down:

1   which predictions of Malthus seem correct?;

2   what developments occurred which Malthus had not been able to take into account?

If you are still uncertain of Malthus's ideas, re-read the section 'Malthus and his ideas on population', above.

Specimen Answers   1   I would note the following predictions of Malthus:
   (a)   Malthus's analysis related to conditions in Europe in 1800 where the population had been growing at a fast rate since the middle of the century. The increase in the birth rate in England caused by the lowering of the age of marriage, at the end of the century and in the early years of the nineteenth century, does seem to coincide with Malthus's prediction that 'population increases where the means of subsistence increase'.
   (b)   The same might be said for the increase in the birth rate, discernible in many countries around the middle of the century.
   (c)   The relatively late age of marriage in Europe and the high percentage of those within the community who did not marry, corresponds with what Malthus would regard as the most highly approved of preventive checks – moral restraint.

(d)   This is particularly noticeable in France where from the very start of the century it is clear that generations of Frenchmen and women deliberately restricted the size of their families.

(e)   The high ceiling of preventive checks is seen in the last decades of the nineteenth century when birth rates fall, at a time when the means of subsistence is increasing. The Malthusian lesson of moral restraint, together with forms of contraception (in Malthus's eyes – vice) was helping to ensure growing wealth and rising standards of living.

2   Malthus's gloomy forecast, that population grows in a geometrical ratio while food supplies only increase in an arithmetical ratio, was nullified with improvements in transport and a rapidly increasing food supply with the importation of food and cereals from overseas.

Death rates in the nineteenth century

Perhaps it is stating the obvious to point out that if the population of Europe kept increasing throughout the century and, for the most part, the birth rate fell during the course of the century, then in order to account for this increase the fall in the death rate must have been occurring at a faster rate and, indeed, that was the case.

Exercise   Have a look at the death rate statistics in Table 3. What countries have the lowest death rates over this period?

Specimen Answers   You will probably have noted the following.

1   The pattern is fairly similar to that relating to birth rates. Generally speaking, the death rate becomes higher the further east one goes. Rates in southern Europe are also high compared with the northern countries.

2   Death rates declined in many countries in the period 1831–5 to 1841–5 but the decline is not sustained. In the last decades of the century, especially the period 1891–1900, death rates fall markedly in most countries, eastern as well as western, and southern as well as northern. Note that this marked fall coincides with the fall in the birth rate which affects virtually all European countries by the end of the century.

What is clear is that death rates were falling in many countries from the start of our period, especially in Western Europe and Scandinavia. It is

Table 3: Death Rates in Europe 1801–99 : per 1,000 Population

	1801–5	1811–5	1821–5	1831–5	1841–5	1851–5	1861–5	1871–5	1881–5	1891–5	1896–99
Norway	24.1	23.4	18.7	20.1	17.4	17.3	18.6	17.5	17.1	16.9	15.7
Sweden	24.4	27.0	22.1	23.8	20.2	21.7	19.8	18.3	17.6	16.6	16.0
France	29.3	26.9	24.8	25.6	22.7	24.1	23.0	24.9	22.2	22.3	20.3
Germany			24.1	28.7	26.0	27.1	26.0	28.2	25.8	23.3	21.1
Austria			27.0	34.1	30.6	34.2	30.0	32.6	30.2	27.8	25.4
Belgium				26.1	23.5	22.0	22.8	23.4	21.1	20.3	17.8
Denmark	24.3	24.1	20.0	25.8	19.6	20.3	20.2	19.5	18.4	18.6	16.3
Finland	24.7	28.1	25.7	31.5	22.2	28.2	25.8	21.6	22.2	20.7	18.6
England & Wales					21.4	22.7	22.6	21.9	19.4	18.7	17.6
Bulgaria										28.0	24.5
Hungary							31.9	45.4	33.3	31.9	28.0
Ireland								18.3	18.3	18.5	16.7
Romania							24.5	31.3	26.3	31.0	28.2
Russia							36.8	37.1	36.4	36.2	32.4
Serbia							32.6	32.9	24.5	28.9	25.2
Spain							29.7		32.6	30.3	28.8
Switzerland								23.8	21.2	19.8	17.9
Scotland							22.2	22.7	19.6	19.0	17.8

Source: Mitchell, 1992

also clear that the major reason for this fall was the reduction in deaths from infectious diseases. But the reasons why and how their reduction was brought about are hotly debated by historians and demographers. What is evident is that there is no monocausal factor which satisfactorily explains the fall. For example, the bubonic plague was eliminated from Europe by the early years of the nineteenth century. The various reasons given for this are: the build up within humans of a resistance to the plague as a result of better nutrition: a weakening of the virulence of the plague bacillus, perhaps as a result of climatic changes or, in this instance, a change within the rodent population and the replacement of the black by the brown rat; the replacement of brick for lath and plaster built houses; the development of European border controls and in particular the growing efficiency of the Habsburg government in supervising the overland trade routes from the east and Middle East; more awareness of the need for and more efficient methods of public quarantine.

All these explanations can be examined under the following headings and we will look at each of them in turn:

- advances in medical science;

- better nutrition;

- improved living conditions;

- a decrease in the virulence of some infectious diseases.

Advances in medical science

Smallpox, a major killer disease in earlier centuries, was largely eliminated in Britain by the early years of the nineteenth century as a result of inoculation and vaccination. Other countries took early action against smallpox and compulsory vaccination was introduced in Bavaria in 1806, Hesse in 1807, Norway and Sweden in 1810 and Baden in 1815, but in France it was delayed until almost a century later (1902).

Cholera was much more difficult to eliminate. Epidemics occurred throughout the century, particularly in 1831–2, 1835–7, 1848, 1854–5, 1866–7 (the last major epidemic in Britain), 1872–3 (where it is estimated that some 300,000 people in Hungary died), 1884 in France and 1892 in Germany (some 8,000 deaths in just one city, Hamburg).

The threat of cholera and smallpox, quite understandably, spread fear into the hearts of nineteenth-century communities. Nevertheless, from the point of view of the overall demography of Europe, McKeown (1976, p.88) has argued that 'the occasional epidemic infections contributed much less to the general level of mortality than the endemic diseases which killed the majority of all live-born individuals before they reached maturity'.

During this century, as opposed to previous ones, much more time and money was spent on improving medical facilities. The number of hospitals in Prussia increased from 155 in 1822 to 684 in 1855. The first fever hospital opened in Ireland at the end of the eighteenth century; by the 1840s there were over 100 in the country (cited in Tranter, 1985, p.69). In England there were 33 voluntary hospitals at the start of the century, by 1891 there were 385. The use of anaesthetics in the 1840s and the application of antiseptics in the 1860s contributed vastly to the development of surgery. But most historians doubt whether improved medical services had any appreciable effect on the reduction of the death rate, at least until the last years of the nineteenth century. Indeed, McKeown (1976, p.78) argues that apart from the introduction of inoculation and vaccination against smallpox, 'the role of medical innovation in falling mortality ... between the mid-eighteenth and mid-nineteenth centuries ... was of relatively little value'.

Better nutrition

As we shall see in the next unit, during the nineteenth century there was an immense increase in the food supply due to a number of factors. But subsistence crises were not entirely eliminated. The enormous dust cloud arising from a volcanic eruption in Indonesia caused harvest failures in much of Europe during 1816–17. Germany, Switzerland, the Habsburg Empire and Spain were particularly badly hit and deaths caused by a shortage of food and a consequent weakening of resistance to disease, were high.

Again, in 1846–7 there were very poor harvests and potato crop failures, particularly in parts of Germany and Ireland. The potato, with its high yield per acre compared with grain, was the staple diet for the Irish. Its use meant that families could exist on much smaller plots of land than if they were dependent on grain crops. This increase of their food supply, it is believed, encouraged earlier marriages and the population of Ireland doubled from 4 million to 8 million between 1781 and 1841. The failure of the potato crop had a devastating effect. Estimates of the number of deaths resulting from the famine vary but it was probably in the region of around 750,000. Many more people left the country. The total population fell and it was a fall which continued throughout the century as numbers of emigrants remained high, the age of marriage rose and a high percentage of the population remained unmarried.

Harvest failures later on in the century hit those countries and areas which were comparatively isolated and where transport routes were poor. In this respect it was southern and eastern Europe which suffered most. Spain was particularly badly hit in 1856–7. Even by the end of the century subsistence crises had not been entirely eliminated. Russia suffered a severe famine in 1891–2.

Although, in one sense, the potato was the villain in the Irish famine of 1846/7, its introduction has been seen as an important factor in improving levels of nutrition in the nineteenth century. Fridlizius (1979, p.349) finds a connection in Sweden, where potato output rose sixfold between 1800–10 and 1820–30, between improved and more plentiful diets and a decline in the mortality rate. Flinn (1977), also argues that the development of potato cultivation in Scotland in the second half of the eighteenth century, was an important factor in the decline in the death rate. But the potato should not claim all the credit. Areas where grain production increased significantly, such as in Denmark, also witnessed declines in mortality rates. Although, this is not the case in the agricultural provinces of East Prussia where agricultural improvements occurred but where above average mortality rates were still recorded (Lee, 1979, p.16).

Nevertheless, it would be extremely unwise to argue against the premise that the general increase in agricultural productivity together with rises in real wages, which enabled people to enjoy better diets, resulted in them being more able to resist infectious diseases. Also, if they were more resistant to infections, the chances of these infections being spread were lessened (McKeown, 1976).

Anderson, in his brief survey of population changes, states that the 'most striking feature' of mortality rates in the nineteenth century was the decline in the death rate of young children. He cites the greater availability of cows' milk, especially in north-west Europe as a major factor in this improvement. Certainly, right at the very end of the period (but not until into the twentieth century for some countries) there was a sharp decline in infant mortality rates and increased supplies of milk, together with improved methods for processing and storing it, are important factors in explaining this fall.

Improvements in living conditions

There is no doubt that by the end of the period improvements in living conditions were important factors in reducing mortality rates in many parts of Europe. In Unit 5 David Englander discusses the improvements made in public health, housing and welfare provision. He points out that there were marked divergences in provision from country to country and that for much of the century, with the rapid growth of industrial and urban centres, environmental conditions deteriorated. Tainted water supplies, absence of efficient sewage systems, inadequate housing, and vast overcrowding, meant that epidemics of water, air and food-borne diseases spread quickly. Life expectancy in towns was usually lower than in rural areas. In 1880 the average life expectancy of a person living in Berlin was just under 30 years while in the rural areas of Hanover it was over 43 years. In the early years of the century, while the death rate in the rural areas of Sweden was 22.3 per thousand, in Stockholm it was 45.1. Similar contrasts can be made between rural and city areas in every country of Europe and also between socio-occupational groupings, where life expectancy among the professional classes was much higher than among town labourers.

From the second half of the century onwards, improvements in water supplies, sewage systems, better housing, less overcrowding, and improved personal cleanliness, all contributed towards a decline in the death rates. In Britain, 'the rate of decline of mortality before the turn of the century, was much greater for the enteric diseases, then spread mainly by water, than for the diarrhoeal diseases spread by food' (McKeown, 1976, p.61). There is no reason to believe that this was not the case in other European countries.

A decrease in the virulence of infectious diseases

It is difficult to disentangle separate explanations for the decline in the death rate over this period. For example, was better nutrition, a key factor in increasing people's resistance to infectious diseases, more important? How can these two factors be assessed separately? McKeown (1976) does discuss the possible lessening of the virulence of these diseases – typhus and scarlet fever – in the nineteenth century, but there is no significant evidence to support the theory. The same goes for the suggestion that climatic changes were an important factor in the decline in mortality. This is explored by Wrigley and Schofield (1981) in relation to England.

Exercise   Now for an exercise similar to the one undertaken at the end of the previous section when we reviewed the section on birth rates by examining developments in relation to Malthus's ideas which he put forward at the start of the century. Which predictions of Malthus seem correct when looking at the reasons for the fluctuations in mortality rates in the nineteenth century?

Specimen Answers   1   Rapidly growing population increases in some countries were halted by what Malthus called positive checks. That is, the spread of epidemics and famine. For example, Ireland underwent a population explosion in the first four decades of the century, but was beset by a potato failure in 1846 which led to many deaths, many more people fleeing the country and a drastic drop in the total population of the country.

2   The argument that the fall in the mortality rate was due to increased food supplies and better nutrition, fits snugly into the Malthusian hypothesis that population increases where the means of subsistence increase.

Conclusions

Compared with those in 1800, the people living in Europe at the end of the century, were healthier and lived longer. But there were marked differences in the state of health and life expectancy from country to country and within countries and between different socio-occupational groupings. Nevertheless, as a result of better diets, rising standards of living, improved hygiene, and medical advances, the threat of death as a result of the spread of a large number of infectious diseases was reduced. What is clear, is that during this century much more time and resources were spent on attempting to reduce mortality rates than in previous centuries. Just why this was the case must be connected in some ways with the growth of industrialization and urban living but its links with political and military factors are well worth exploration.

Emigration

One safety-valve by which population pressures were eased in the nineteenth century and which was not considered by Malthus in the extract that we looked at, was migration. Migration takes three forms: migration within the country of origin, migration from one part of Europe to another, and migration out of Europe to other continents. The first of these forms will be discussed in Unit 9 which deals with industrialization. (See also Video 2.) The second will be touched on below but the bulk of this section will deal with emigration from Europe between 1800 and 1900.

Somewhere in the region of 40 million people (roughly equal to the population of England, Scotland and Wales in 1900) emigrated from Europe to various parts of the world during this period. The numbers of emigrants increased throughout the century, partly because of internal population pressures and partly as a result of transport becoming quicker, cheaper and more readily available. In the period from 1821 to 1850 an average of 110,000 persons per year emigrated from Europe; by the end of the century the number had arisen to around 900,000 per year.

The points of destination for these immigrants were mainly to the New World and particularly the United States of America. During the period 1815–1930, the USA received some 33 million immigrants, Argentina 6 million, Canada 5 million, Brazil 4 million and Australia 3.5 million (Baines, 1991, p.8).

As well as having important economic and social effects on both Europe and the receiving countries, this high level of emigration led, as Baines (1991, pp.11–12) has pointed out, to a marked 'redistribution of the European population. Only 4 per cent of ethnic Europeans were living outside Europe and Siberia around 1800. By the First World War this proportion was 21 per cent and rising.'

Table 4: Overseas Emigration. European Countries (1914 boundaries), 1851–1930

Annual average rate per 1000 population

	1851–60	1861–70	1871–80	1881–90	1891–00	1901–10
Ireland	14.0	14.6	6.6	14.2	8.9	7.0
Norway	2.4	5.8	4.7	9.5	4.5	8.3
Scotland	5.0	4.6	4.7	7.1	4.4	9.9
Italy			1.1	3.4	5.0	10.8
England	2.6	2.8	4.0	5.6	3.6	5.5
Sweden	0.5	3.1	2.4	7.0	4.1	4.2
Portugal		1.9	2.9	3.8	5.1	5.7
Spain				3.6	4.4	5.7
Denmark			2.1	3.9	2.2	2.8
Finland				1.3	2.3	5.5
Austria-Hungary			0.3	1.1	1.6	4.8
Switzerland			1.3	3.2	1.4	1.4
Germany			1.5	2.9	1.0	0.5
Netherlands	0.5	0.6	0.5	1.2	0.5	0.5
Belgium				0.9	0.4	0.6
France	0.1	0.2	0.2	0.3	0.1	0.1

Source: Baines, 1991

Exercise   From your knowledge of the condition of Europe in the nineteenth century and from what you have read so far in this unit, what were the major factors in persuading people to emigrate?

Specimen Answers   1   Unemployment, poor prospects for employment, and depressed living conditions.

2   Crisis conditions such as famine.

3   Political and religious persecution.
(These are all factors commonly known as 'push' factors, i.e. when conditions are so bad that there is a strong incentive to 'get away from it all'.)

4   Another important factor for emigration, and full marks if you have thought of it, is the belief, on the part of those contemplating emigration, that prospects for work and higher living standards are better at the place of destination than at home. (This is what is known as a 'pull' factor.)

Exercise   Look at Table 4 relating to overseas emigration from European countries, 1851–60 to 1901–10.

What are the major trends in the rates of emigration from individual countries during this period?

Specimen Answers   1   Throughout this period Ireland has an extremely high proportion of emigrants.

2   By the start of the second half of the century emigration is an important factor in regard to Scotland and much of Scandinavia.

3   In the decade 1881–90, partly as transport becomes cheaper and more frequent, emigration rates rise for most countries, particularly Sweden and Norway.

4   By the end of the century the numbers leaving southern Europe – Spain, Portugal and particularly Italy, are rising. (In the decade 1901–10 over 1 in every 100 Italians leave the country.) Also, not shown in this table, there is a large amount of emigration, particularly of Jewish and Polish minorities, from the Russian Empire.

5   The numbers emigrating from France remain at a low level throughout the century. Clearly, with its low population growth France was not facing the internal pressures common to most other European countries.

In many ways, the trends in the rate of emigration mirror the rates of population increase in Europe. That is, for the earlier part of the century the rates are high in western Europe (excepting France), but by the end of the century, the rates in southern and eastern Europe are increasing rapidly.

Reasons for emigration

Depressed conditions

Emigration from Europe was not a unique nineteenth-century phenomenon. Unspecified numbers had moved to the Americas from the sixteenth century onwards. However in Britain, in the years immediately following the ending of the Napoleonic Wars, during periods of agricultural depression and industrial unemployment the number of emigrants increased rapidly. Emigration was one of the few solutions that contemporary commentators advocated for what some of them thought was an 'overpopulation problem'. In order to carry out this solution a number of private emigration schemes were launched as well as public ones. In the years between 1815 and 1826 six state-aided emigration schemes were introduced by successive governments (Tranter, 1985, p.129).

The numbers involved in these state schemes were relatively small compared with private emigration (about 1 in 5) but most of them were aimed at relieving distress in particular potential trouble-spots in the country. One scheme, introduced in 1819 soon after the Peterloo incident, involved a government grant-aided plan to induce people to emigrate to the Cape of Good Hope. The government guaranteed a boat passage and 100 acres of land for every emigrant family. In return, those hoping to make the trip were asked to lay down a deposit of £10, which would cover costs for a husband, wife and two children under 14. An extra £5 was demanded for every extra 2 children and £5 for every person between 14 and 18. In Nottingham, where unemployment, particularly among framework knitters, was high, the government's scheme was welcomed and the money to cover the deposits of would-be emigrants was raised by a local appeal launched by the Lord Lieutenant of the county. Eventually sufficient money was raised to provide for 158 people from Nottinghamshire to make the journey (60 men, 26 women and 72 children under eighteen years of age). Of the 60 men, 17 were framework knitters and 16 others were recorded as labourers. Once a boat provided by the navy was ready to take them to the Cape, the emigrants made their way to Liverpool, the men on foot and the women in wagons (Notts C.R.O. CP5/1 Undated circular headed Downing Street 1819 and Notts C.R.O. CP5/1 30 January returns of settlers going to the Cape of Good Hope).

Later on, with the setting up on the new Poor Law administration in 1834, new schemes were introduced which enabled a further 25,000 people, mainly agricultural labourers from the southern counties of England, to emigrate between 1834 and 1860.

Exercise Look at Document II.2 and read the letter from Mr Pinnock to the Poor Law Commissioners dated 12 July 1836 together with that of Mr Buchanan. What do they see as the relevant 'push' and 'pull' factors determining emigration?

Specimen Answers   1   Push factors involve unemployment and poor conditions at home.

2   Financial support towards their passages to Canada and the prospect of work and good wages on reaching their destination are important pull factors.

Other governments in western Europe introduced similar schemes, especially in the early years of the century. But as emigration became more acceptable and as the numbers of emigrants increased each year, the need for governments to encourage potential emigrants lessened and many schemes were dropped or taken over by private rail and land companies. However, in Britain in particular, there was one further reason why the government wished to continue such schemes. This related to the need to populate her colonies. As the letter from Mr Pinnock reveals, this was no major problem in relation to Canada because the costs of transporting emigrants was relatively low, but in order to persuade local authorities to inaugurate similar schemes to Australia and New Zealand, the government was forced to subsidize the travelling expenses to these lands.

Despite all these schemes, it has been estimated that only around 10 per cent of all European emigrants received official assistance. The vast majority paid their own fares or were assisted financially by friends and relations (Baines, 1991, p.50).

It seems clear from this evidence that poor conditions at home were factors in accounting for emigration from Europe. However, if depressed conditions were a major factor, then we would expect emigration rates to be inversely related to the economic development of these countries. Although this is true of some countries with high per capita incomes such as Belgium and the Netherlands, and in Germany where there was a marked decline in emigration at the end of the century which coincided with rapid industrialization, it was not always the case. Of course, as Baines (1991, p.25) has pointed out, 'the majority of European emigrants were poor or came from rural areas since these were the characteristics of a high proportion of the European population' but in Britain emigration rates rose, or remained high as economic conditions improved and internal standards of living rose. Baines also cites Carlsson who found no close relationship between emigration and economic and social conditions in Sweden. In addition, within particular countries, the rates of emigration vary widely from area to area. In Italy the rural regions of Calabria, the Arbruzzi, Sicily, Emilio-Romagnia and Sardinia were equally poor, but the emigration rates were around eight to ten times higher in the first three than in the last two (Baines, 1991, p.32).

Apart from poor living conditions, one further explanation for high numbers emigrating from a particular region of a country is the factor of continuity or 'chain migration'. That is, the first wave of emigrants, in writing home to relatives and friends, often encouraged them to make the journey to the new homeland (Erickson, 1972a). So, other members of the family or the same community would also emigrate, often to the same area as the original settlers. As Baines (1991, p.33) writes, for most people it was more reassuring to move from 'the known to the known'. Around 70 per cent of all Norwegians who emigrated from Europe, settled in just six states of the USA, and, by 1914, over one-quarter of the million and a half Italian immigrants in the USA lived in New York.

Famine

The emigration push factor can best be traced at times of acute harvest failure. The peaking of emigration figures from Germany in 1816–7, 1847 and 1853 coincide with either serious harvest failures or potato blight (Lee, 1979). Some 935,000 people emigrated from southern Germany during the famine of 1847 and even more emigrated from Ireland where the potato blight had such disastrous consequences. As well as hundreds of thousands dying, well over 1.6 million emigrated from Ireland during the period 1847 to 1854. Emigration figures in Ireland remained high for the rest of the century as agricultural changes in that country reduced the demand for labour.

As the century progressed so there were fewer major famines, but emigration rates remained high in those rural areas of Europe where agricultural lands were subdivided among families, such as in Ireland, south-west Germany and parts of Poland, Portugal, Germany and Italy.

Political and religious persecution

The threat of religious persecution was another emigration push factor. Minority religious groups left Germany in large numbers in the 1830s and there were similar movements away from Norway and Sweden in the 1850s. The mass migration from eastern Europe in the 1880s was dominated by the fear of political and religious persecution. Towards the end of the century especially, Poles and Jews from both Russia and Austria emigrated to the United States in vast numbers. But in all these cases, although the original reason for emigration was persecution or the threat of persecution, the chain factor must also be taken into account. The original persecuted emigrants made it easier for people of similar religious beliefs or ethnic origins to emigrate but the motivations of these later emigrants might well have been different.

Changes in emigration

During the nineteenth century the nature of emigration changed in a number of respects. First, the early emigrants often consisted of young families. By the end of the century, the proportion of single males emigrating had risen and there were twice as many men emigrating as women. Again there are exceptions to this. Throughout the century there was always a higher proportion of men to women amongst Swedish emigrants, while there was always a high proportion of female emigrants from Ireland. Low marriage rates and lack of job opportunities after the Irish famine, meant that Irish women (who also had the advantage of being English speaking) found better prospects both in the labour and marriage markets in the United States.

One of the reasons for the switch from family to individual emigration was a change in the pull factor. Opportunities for agricultural workers, which seemed so plentiful in 1820 were not so apparent in 1900. As we saw with our examples from England in 1820 and the 1830s, land was made available to settlers, but by the end of the century, Canada was the only country where it was relatively easy to buy a family farm. Of course, there were job opportunities for farm labourers in the New World but the major demand was for labour in industrial areas.

Secondly, as the century went on, an increasing number of emigrants returned to Europe. It has been estimated that altogether about one in four of all emigrants returned to Europe. Around 40 per cent of the English and Welsh who emigrated in the period 1861–1913 made the return journey and 50 per cent of Italians returned from Argentina and the United States over the same period (Gould, 1980).

The return rate of emigrants increased during the century as travel became cheaper and easier. In the 1820s and 1830s passage by sailing ship from Liverpool to New York, which took any time between three and ten weeks, was hazardous and costly. It has been estimated that 1.5 per cent of emigrants from European ports to New York died during or immediately after these voyages. Also, a single fare was around the equivalent of two months income for an unskilled worker.

With the development of railways, the introduction of steam ships, and the development of shipping companies catering for the emigration trade, travel became comparatively easy and Erickson (1972b, p.371–3) has shown that a considerable proportion of men travelling from Britain to the United States in the 1880s, were either commercial men or building workers who were seeking seasonal work in New York. The men in both these categories had no intention of remaining permanently abroad. The same can be said for many of the emigrants from southern and eastern Europe. The aim of a sizeable proportion of Italian emigrants was to make enough money abroad so that they could return and buy a plot of land in their place of origin.

Inter-European migration

By no means all emigration involved travel outside Europe. Many of the Poles and Jews escaping from Russia in the 1880s moved westward and settled in other European countries. The number of Jews in Britain rose from 60,000 in 1881 to around 300,000 by the outbreak of the First World War, largely as a result of this migration westward. Again, many of the Irish escaping the Famine in the 1840s turned towards England and Scotland as well as America. By 1851, some 7.2 per cent of the population of Scotland was made up of people born in Ireland (Flinn, 1977, p.457).

With the development of industrialization, particularly in western Europe, there were increasing opportunities for movements from country to country. The industrial area of the Ruhr attracted workers particularly from countries in the east. France, too, attracted immigrants. In fact, towards the end of the century its population increase was largely accounted for by immigrants mainly from Italy (over 600,000 between 1866 and 1906). Seasonal migration was also an important factor. For generations peasants from northern Italy travelled to Austria, France and Switzerland to work on building sites (perhaps precursors to the seasonal traffic of building workers to and from the United States). France also benefited from seasonal migration, with labourers coming across the borders in the north to help with the beet harvest and Italians coming in from the south to work in the vineyards. In the north of Norway some 30,000 men migrated to the fishing areas of the Lofoten Islands from January to April each year. This was such a high proportion of the male – and married – population that it had a noticeably marked effect on the timing of conceptions!

The relationships between population changes and the economic and social life of Europe

At the outset of this unit I stated that I considered demographic change to be the most fundamental and important factor in the history of Europe in the nineteenth century. The consequences on a continent, where the population more than doubled in the space of one hundred years, were bound to be widespread. Yet, perhaps surprisingly, there has been comparatively little research undertaken into evaluating the effects of demographic factors on a whole host of important areas, for example, on the political systems of Europe, on the balance of power within Europe, or of its effect on social policies in European countries. Nevertheless, in this unit and, in the extract that we looked at in Anderson, references have been made to the relationships between population changes and the economic development and social life of Europe.

Exercise From your reading of this unit and from Anderson (pp. 121–4) jot down the areas in which you think population growth affected social and economic life in Europe in the nineteenth century.

Specimen Answers 1 By the beginning of the nineteenth century the population of Europe, especially western Europe was growing rapidly. This population growth put enormous pressures on the level of internal demand and there was increased and improved agricultural activity.

2 Improved agricultural productivity and rises in real wages affected marriage and birth rates.

3 Rural areas were unable to accommodate the enormous growth in the population. Demographic changes were associated with the break up of old agrarian systems.

4 Population growth resulted in increased levels of internal mobility. A discussion concerning the growth of towns occurs later in this block but the volume of population in these areas created demands for the need to improve among other things, medical facilities, water supplies, sewage systems, and housing.

5 The decline of the birth rate at the end of the century reflects changes in family structures and customs. In particular, whereas children were looked upon as part of the family economic unit in many areas of Europe for most of the century, by the last decades this was tending not to be the case.

6   The emigration of over 40 million Europeans during this period to different parts of the world strengthened Europe's position in the world. Emigration also played an important role in the economic development of the receiving countries.

7   Anderson, argues that by the end of the century Europe had reached a stage of demographic development which was extremely favourable for economic developments. The proportion of European populations in active working age groups was high and the fall in death rates had not produced a sizeable percentage of the population who were too old to work. This demographic factor formed the basis for increased economic activity and developments which, he concludes, 'were in many ways strongly favourable to a growth of production and a general rise in living standards' (p.124).

8   Finally, to return to a point which I introduced at the start of this unit. Demographic changes had important diplomatic and military implications. A major reason for Napoleon's success was that at the time he was fighting his battles, one in four Europeans was a Frenchman. But France's low birth rate in the nineteenth century had its effect and by the time of the Franco-Prussian war of 1870, Napoleon III found that demographic trends had stacked the pack against him. From a military point of view worse was to follow. By 1910 France had a population of which some 12.8 per cent was over 60 years of age and 22.5 per cent under 15. Germany, on the other hand, had only 8.5 per cent of her population over 60 and, with a much higher birth rate, 34.1 per cent under 15. The population of the Balkans and Russia in the meantime was soaring. These demographic features, were to have extremely serious political and military consequences which became increasingly apparent in the early years of the twentieth century. In addition, we must not forget the European populations who had migrated overseas and who, as events turned out, played crucial roles in both the two World Wars in the twentieth century.

References

(For those of you who have the time and wish to undertake further reading, the books asterisked below provide interesting and useful introductions to the subject.)

*Anderson, M. (1980), *Approaches to the History of the Western Family 1500–1914*, Macmillan, London and Basingstoke.

*Baines, D. (1991), *Emigration from Europe 1815–1930*, Macmillan, Basingstoke.

Banks, J. A. (1981), *Victorian Values. Secularism and the size of Families*, Routledge and Kegan Paul, London.

Barker, T. and Drake, M. (1982), *Population and Society in Britain 1850–1980*, Batsford, London.

Caron, F. (1979), *An Economic History of Modern France*, Methuen, London.

Drake, M. (1969), *Population and Society in Norway, 1735–1865*, Cambridge University Press, Cambridge.

Drake, M. (1972), 'Fertility controls in pre-industrial Norway' in D.V. Glass and R. Revelle (eds), *Population and Social Change*, Arnold, London.

Erickson, C. J. (1972a), *Invisible Immigrants: the adaptation of English and Scottish immigrants in nineteenth-century America*, Weidenfeld and Nicolson, London.

Erickson, C. J. (1972b), 'Who were the English and Scots immigrants to the United States in the late nineteenth century?' in D.V. Glass, and R. Revelle (eds), *Population and Social Changes*, Arnold, London.

Finnegan, R. and Drake, M. (1994), *Studying Family and Community History, Volume I, From Family Tree to Family History*, Cambridge University Press, Cambridge.

Flinn, M. (ed.) (1977), *Scottish Population History from the Seventeenth Century to the 1930s*, Cambridge University Press, Cambridge.

Fridlizius, G. (1979), 'Sweden' in W.R. Lee (ed.), *European Demography and Economic Growth*, Croom Helm, London.

Gildea, R. (1987), *Barricades and Borders Europe 1800–1914*. Oxford University Press, Oxford.

Gould, J. D. (1980), 'European inter-continental emigration, 1815–1914. The road home: return migration from the USA', *Journal of European Economic History*, 9.

Hajnal, H. J. (1965), 'European marriage patterns in Perspective' in D.V.C. Glass and D.C. Eversley (eds), *Population in History: Essays in Historical Demography*, Edward Arnold, London.

Hobsbawm, E. J. (1962), *The Age of Revolution 1789–1848*, Mentor Books, New York.

Lee, R. (1981), 'Family and "Modernisation". The Peasant Family and Social Change in Nineteenth-century Bavaria', in R. J. Evans and W. R. Lee (eds), *The German Family: Essays on the Social History of the Family in Nineteenth and Twentieth-Century Germany*, Croom Helm, London.

Lee, W. R. (ed.) (1979), *European Demography and Economic Growth*, Croom Helm, London.

Macfarlane, A. (1986), *Marriage and Love in England: Modes of Reproduction 1300–1840*, Basil Blackwell, Oxford.

McKeown, T. (1976), *The Modern Rise of Population*, Arnold, London.

Mitchell, B. R. (1992), *International Historical Statistics Europe 1750–1988*, 3rd edn, Macmillan, London.

*Tranter, N. L. (1985), *Population and Society 1750–1940*, Longman, London.

van der Walle, E. (1979), 'France' in W. R. Lee (ed.) *European Demography and Economic Growth*, Croom Helm, London.

Wrigley, E. A. and Schofield, R. S. (1981), *The Population History of England 1541–1871: A Reconstruction*, Arnold, London.

Unit 8
The transformation of agriculture

Prepared for the course team by Ian Donnachie

Contents

Study timetable

Weeks of study	Texts	Video	AC
2	Unit 8; Offprint 6; Documents II.3–II.9; Anderson		

Aims

The aims of this unit are to encourage you to think about:

1   how European agriculture developed during the nineteenth century;

2   what systems of land tenure, labour and technology prevailed in different parts of Europe;

3   how and why these changed over time;

4   to what extent the systems of land tenure (and agriculture itself) affected the structure of nation states, and by extension, the role of the traditional landowners in the states of Europe;

5   how agriculture and agricultural tariff policies affected economic development generally.

Introduction

European agricultural development, like economic development generally, was highly regional, the timing and pace of modernization in different states reflecting relative progress or backwardness. The great regional differences which existed – even within countries – were primarily functions of topography and climate which directly affected land use everywhere. But they also reflected varied patterns of land ownership, different forms of land tenure, and different farming techniques and products. In short, there were enormous regional variations in the way the land was owned and used – and this makes it difficult to generalize, even within the different states of Europe. For example, while Document II.5, which we will examine later, positively glows with how well French agriculture was doing in 1881, there were mountainous, isolated and mainly pastoral regions of France (the Massif Central, the Alps and the Pyrenees) where resources were inadequate given population pressure and the lack of local industry. Even well-developed countries of the west had their primitive and backward areas.

At the beginning of the nineteenth century, and despite industrialization, much of Europe was still overwhelmingly agrarian. A large proportion of the population – more than four-fifths in some countries, like Russia, Spain, or Italy – was engaged in primary production and still working in conditions of relentless toil that had been the norm of the peasantry for generations. Family labour was universal and women and children worked at the same tasks as men. In parts of central and eastern Europe and in Russia serfdom still prevailed; while elsewhere feudal obligation had long been swept away to be replaced by wage labour paid partly in kind and partly in money.

Substantial areas of Europe were owned and farmed by the traditional landowners, such as the Junkers in Prussia, who though strongly conservative in outlook politically, were also very commercially minded and jealous of their position and interests as agricultural producers. Many of the Junker holdings, perhaps even the majority, were paltry compared with those of the 'improving' gentry in Britain. There commercialization had probably been taken furthest, and the British model had later been copied throughout much of the West, for example in Belgium, France, Germany, the Netherlands, Scandinavia, Italy and elsewhere. Some landowners had rationalized their holdings by selling off portions of their estates or leasing land to others. The latter development created the tenant farmer, who in some contexts had proved a prime mover in the modernization of agriculture. Successful tenant farmers sometimes ended up as landowners themselves. In some contexts, as in much of France following the Revolution, and in Germany, many estates had been broken up and fallen into the hands of a peasant proprietorial class. The sale and lease of larger holdings and the consequent withdrawal of communal rights had also helped to create a landless labouring class. Almost everywhere the landless were beginning to grow in numbers, forcing migration from rural to urban areas or emigration overseas.

With such a large proportion of the population dependent upon agriculture for their means of subsistence, harvest failures could have disastrous social consequences (see Anderson, pp.82–4) as they did in the 1810s (and later in the 1840s when the potato crop failed calamitously in Ireland, the Scottish Highlands and other parts of northern Europe). In this respect the mid-nineteenth century can be seen as a watershed, for thereafter, excepting in Russia, there were few major famines caused by harvest failure. Partly this was a reflection of Europe's enhanced agricultural productivity, its increasing integration into the international primary product market, and of the ability to import food more readily and more cheaply from its periphery, particularly Russia, or from areas of recent settlement and extensive agriculture such as North and South America and Australasia. The high level of imports ultimately reduced farm prices and helped to bring long-term depression to parts of European agriculture. Some states responded to the crises by raising tariffs against imports to protect their own farmers; while some farmers diversified into other forms of agriculture or got together in co-operatives to market their products more effectively.

The growth of the agricultural market

During the nineteenth century, as John Golby explained in Unit 7, the population of Europe, despite massive emigration, more than doubled to reach over 400 million. I would like you to think about the implications this large population increase had for agriculture both in Europe and beyond.

Exercise Re-read Anderson, pp.121–4, then answer the following questions.

1   What was the likely economic impact of population growth on agriculture?

2   How do you think agriculture would fit into the pattern of economic growth described in Anderson's last paragraph on p.124?

Specimen Answers 1   Put simply, if there were not to be periodic subsistence crises with people starving as a result, agricultural production would need to expand to meet the demands of a rising population, an increasing proportion of which, in any case, earned its living in non-agrarian and increasingly, urban, industrial occupations. This could be achieved by extending the agricultural area, raising productivity on the existing cultivable land, or by resort to imports from areas of surplus within Europe or of recent settlement such as those mentioned by Anderson (p.121), like the Americas and Australasia. Note that productivity might also be increased by longer working hours or a reduction in living standards on the land, and that a combination of these factors often forced migration to the towns.

2   In theory at least, agriculture would benefit directly from population growth by enhanced demand for its products. Thanks to a growing urban market reached by improved communications agriculture grew more profitable, thus generating capital for re-investment in the land

or investment in industry or transport. Agriculturists also increased their demands for non-agricultural products, hence further stimulating industry. An efficient agriculture was therefore one of the keys to economic growth, and Anderson (p.124) provides a brief but useful comparison of the differing German and French experiences during the nineteenth century.

There's a great deal packed into these responses that you may have overlooked, but don't worry because we are now going to move on to 'unpack' in greater detail the main reasons why the market for agriculture expanded so dramatically during the nineteenth century.

While, as Anderson observes, 'a growing population meant a growing market' the enlargement of the agricultural market was due to a much more complex set of social, economic and political developments. These are all bound up in two related questions: 'why did the market expand?'; and 'how did agriculture respond?'. We cannot expect to find all the answers at this point, but let's explore them in more detail now.

The expanding market

In this section of the unit we will address the question, 'Why did the market expand?'.

Exercise   Apart from population growth, list the main areas of the economy and social development which had a close relationship with agriculture and were likely to generate increased demand for agricultural products.

Discussion   The most obvious are industrialization, urbanization, enhanced standards of living, changing diets, improved transport, which contributed to the growth of national and international markets, and something you would associate more readily with industry, scientific and technological developments.

We shall now examine these points further.

Industrialization

You will be studying this in greater depth in Unit 9, but for the moment it is sufficient to note the close relationship between industrialization and the growth of the market for agricultural products. Clearly, as more and more people moved from primary production to manufacturing – and this was apparent even in the early or 'proto-industrial' phase in most countries – there was a need for increased agricultural output to support the growing industrial workforce. There was also enhanced demand for agricultural raw materials needed in an important group of primary processing industries, such as milling, leather working, soap manufacture, and the drink industries, notably wine production, brewing and distilling. Indeed, these activities are all good examples of consumer industries which in many countries developed rapidly from craft-based activities to mass production during the nineteenth century. Brewing is a good case in point for in both Britain and Germany it developed rapidly into an industry of large-scale urban production units – yet still maintained an intimate contact with the countryside which supplied its raw materials and to which waste was returned for use as animal feed or fertilizer. Quite often these enterprises were partly or wholly financed by successful landowners or farmers. Given the unevenness of industrialization throughout Europe during the nineteenth century the impact on agriculture varied from country to country – but it was felt almost everywhere and such was the growth of demand that it led to greatly increased trade in agricultural products within nation states and across national boundaries.

Urbanization

As was pointed out in Unit 7, the nineteenth century saw an unprecedented growth in towns and cities throughout much of Europe which greatly enlarged the market for food products.

Statistics of proportions of rural–urban populations show the balance moving in favour of town dwellers as the century progressed, notably in the countries affected by industrialization. Of course, this is not to say that all those classified as urban dwellers were necessarily engaged in non-agrarian occupations since many townsfolk and villagers in the more backward areas continued to work the land as they had done for generations. Nevertheless densely populated cities and towns everywhere generated new demands on agriculture.

Around most major cities, London, Paris, Vienna, for example, and industrial areas, like Lancashire, Clydeside, and the Ruhr, agriculture, and particularly horticulture, dairying, poultry, and pig rearing, prospered thanks to the proximity of large and expanding markets.

Enhanced standards of living

While there is continuing debate among historians about the short-term impact of both agrarian reforms and industrialization on the standard of living, and bearing in mind the enormous regional variations, there were undoubtedly improvements in the longer term for at least some of the working class and the majority of the middle class. Increased spending power on the necessities of life – and for some greater luxuries – was therefore another important trigger to improved agricultural productivity.

Changing diets

Changing diet was an important aspect of better standards of living which not only affected overall demand but also the kinds of products demanded by consumers. Among the peasant population of Ireland, Scotland, Germany and Scandinavia the potato became a subsistence crop, while the much superior diet of a more affluent proportion of the population brought about a gradual shift from the consumption of oats and rye to wheat and increased demand for meat, poultry, dairy products, and vegetables.

Improved transport

Like industrial manufactures, agriculture benefited enormously from improved transport, roads, river navigation, canals, shipping and railways. At first these helped to widen local and regional markets, then as networks extended they contributed to the growth of national and then international markets. Clearly export from areas of surplus, such as East Prussia or Hungary, was long established, but improved and cheaper transport offered even greater opportunities. Railways were particularly important in mixed farming areas which specialized in perishables like dairy products, fruit and vegetables that had to get speedily to urban markets. Beyond Europe the transport revolution in steam shipping also helped to open up world markets allowing cheaper importation of cereals, and, thanks to refrigeration, meat products from areas of recent settlement like North America, South America and Australasia. Such imports, increasing in volume as the century progressed, helped feed Europe's rapidly growing population, but depressed agricultural prices at home and caused major problems of adjustment which we will address below.

Scientific and technological developments

Finally, significant developments in science and technology greatly improved food processing and storage. Canning was an early nineteenth-century development, while artificial refrigeration, originally used in breweries to control the fermentation process, was by the 1870s being applied to meat preservation, opening up the market for frozen meat imported from North and South America, Australia and New Zealand. Pasteur's discoveries in the field of bacteriology had an enormous impact on dairying, bringing greater purity and quality control to the products. While such developments were only indirectly triggered by the needs of producers they greatly extended the scope for further expansion of the meat trade and of dairying.

Agriculture's response

In this section we move on to examine how agriculture responded to the expanding market.

Exercise Given the widening market and new opportunities arising during the nineteenth century how do you think agriculture responded?

Discussion The short answer is by improved efficiency. You could expand on this by saying that it invariably involved a shift from subsistence to the market; re-organization of land use and holdings (often at the expense of the peasants who had worked the land for generations); more productive crops and animals; improved husbandry, which sometimes involved new technological or scientific developments; and greater investment of capital.

Many of these developments, which we will look at in greater detail later in the unit, were pioneered in the Netherlands and France before their transfer during the eighteenth century to England where they combined to create the 'Agricultural Revolution'. This was a period of sustained change in land use and of enhanced productivity, described by one historian, Deane (1975, p.50), as 'part and parcel' of the same process that brought about the 'Industrial Revolution'. The English example, though in many ways quite distinctive, was later emulated elsewhere in the British Isles and in Europe, notably in Germany and Scandinavia.

Such responses to fresh opportunities, like the factors influencing increased demand, which we examined above, were closely inter-related, and while the timing differed from one country to another, the pattern of development was roughly comparable.

Despite the changes summarized here we must not forget that much of Europe, particularly the eastern and southern periphery, was little affected and that peasant-based subsistence agriculture with some surplus filtering through to the market, remained the norm into the twentieth century.

The agrarian structure: land ownership, labour, and technology

Here again generalization is dangerous, but, as Anderson (p.183) emphasizes, it is possible to see dramatic changes in some contexts and continuing stagnation in others, the most dynamic areas being in the north west of the continent. This was partly historical and partly the result of industrialization, which, as we saw, generated new demands on agriculture. It's also important to remember that in the new industrial areas agriculture was still important: overall it occupied 90 per cent of usable land.

Land ownership

Patterns of land ownership varied enormously throughout Europe, but everywhere broadly reflected the degree to which elements of the age-old social order with noble landowners dominating the hierarchy had persisted into the nineteenth century. In some contexts even this was hardly an accurate measure of how much the agrarian structure was changing before serfdom was swept away under the emancipation laws, since the progressive commercialization of agriculture had slowly altered the relationship of master and servant.

Exercise Read Anderson pp.183–4, concentrating on his discussion of land ownership in the period 1850–70. What points of comparison and contrast can you see in patterns of land ownership in the various countries mentioned? What factors contributed to change?

Discussion Surprisingly, despite industrialization (and perhaps because of it), Britain was exceptional in Europe because the élite still owned – in large estates of 10,000 acres or more – 25 per cent of the land area. More than 50 per cent of the land was in estates over 1,000 acres, whereas in France such estates represented only 20 per cent of the land. In Russia there were some large estates, but there, as in Prussia, Saxony and Hanover the land held by the nobility was in decline, especially after emancipation. The erosion, as Anderson (p.183) says, was a slow process, explained by industrialization, increased mobility, mass basic education (though not much affecting central and eastern Europe), and peasant demands linked to emancipation. One feature of the British legal system – the entail – though also found in France and Russia, helped keep large estates in the hands of the same families. But, in short, powerful forces of modernization and commercialization were modifying patterns of land ownership and the agrarian structure in many parts of Europe. Anderson provides a useful snapshot of different patterns of land-holding in the mid-nineteenth century, though without telling us much about how these patterns had developed over time.

We can get some insight into the survival of old and new structures alongside one another through a brief examination of the situation in Hanover, a relatively progressive area in northern Germany, during the early nineteenth century.

Exercise   Read Document II.3. What does this tell you about land ownership and agrarian class structure in Hanover in 1820?

Discussion   The main landowners in Hanover were the king, the nobles, the towns and the religious bodies, accounting for five-sixths of the area between them, and with the remaining sixth being in the hands of the non-nobility. Some large land-holdings existed (anything between 500 and 3,000 acres), but generally the majority had been split into smaller holdings of 100–500 acres. Few of the 644 nobles actually cultivated their estates. The majority did not even live on their estates – they were absentee landlords. Smaller land-holdings between 5 and 80 acres were the norm – held under long-established systems of tenure with occupiers paying rent or providing labour services to the owner. Two classes of land-holders are identified here: the *meyer* and the *leibeigner*, both of the peasant class, differentiated mainly by the size of their holding. Their conditions of service varied with status, the *leibeigner* being in virtual serfdom. About 80 per cent of the country was cultivated by these two groups and their families. Lack of capital and feudal services made the system inefficient. Finally, agricultural labourers, common in England, were unusual in Germany.

While the document does not provide any information about change-over time, or the extent to which agricultural production was for the market, it certainly suggests that strong elements of the traditional social order, common to much of central and eastern Europe, still survived in this part of Germany prior to emancipation. It also suggests something that was common in Germany, France and elsewhere, the juxtaposition of large holdings worked on increasingly capitalist lines, mainly devoted to cereals (or vines), set alongside numerous smaller holdings worked by members of the peasant class. In this respect, as Kemp (1985, p.11) observes, what distinguished British, and particularly English, development from continental Europe was the fact that 'feudal agrarian relations', of the kind described in Hanover, 'began to break up earlier and did so more rapidly and completely'. There were many absentee landlords everywhere – not just in Hanover. But this too was traditional and it does not allow us to infer that the new agriculture was of little interest to them – since it was potentially more profitable than the old and assumed greater importance in the economies of individual states as the nineteenth century progressed.

While changing patterns of land-holding were slowly modifying the agrarian structure, creating more tenant farmers and small peasant owners, changes in land use related to the new demands of commercial agriculture, also greatly affected rural dwellers. Again the early experience of Britain indicated a general long-term trend in the reorganization of holdings, enclosure of former open fields, extension of agriculture on to former common lands and wastes, the alienation or elimination of peasant holdings where it conflicted with the interests of capitalist agriculture. The experience of the Highland crofter and the Irish peasant evicted from their holdings during much of the nineteenth century was replicated in many other parts of Europe with the same profound social consequences of landlessness, rural depopulation and migration to the towns or emigration overseas.

Labour

What proportion of the population was engaged in agriculture, what were the characteristics of the peasantry and of rural life, and what changes took place in the status and conditions of labour during the period? Again, in setting out to answer these questions, generalizations present pitfalls for the unwary but we can see the same survival of custom and tradition in some contexts, and important new developments in others. The final breakdown of serfdom emerges as one of the most significant themes in the agrarian history of central and eastern Europe, but again it's easy to exaggerate its immediate impact. In some states, for example in Russia, the abolition of serfdom merely substituted one form of unfree labour for another, ostensibly free, but continuing to exploit peasants through low wages and/or high rents.

In developed societies farming is only one among scores of other forms of employment, but in traditional societies a high proportion of the population was engaged in agriculture. Indeed, as Bairoch (1975, p.467) notes, detailed statistics of employment are a sort of by-product of development, as the following data drawn from the earliest censuses to provide occupations in different states show.

Exercise   Examine and comment upon the data presented in Table 1. What are the dangers in taking such statistics at face value?

Discussion   Despite the chronological differences in the data, and some reservations about the accuracy of the data, particularly for Germany, the most obvious point that can be made about them is that they show the continuing dominance of agriculture as a major means of employment. Broadly speaking in ranking the data the least industrialized countries, for example, those on the periphery like Poland, Russia and Spain, had the highest levels of agricultural employment, while, not surprisingly, the more industrialized like

Table 1: Percentage of working population employed in agriculture from earliest available censuses

Country	Date	Percentage
Austria	1869	68
Belgium	1846	51
Denmark	1850	60
Finland	[1754]	82
France	1856	54
Germany	1882	47
Great Britain	1841	26
Hungary	1857	74
Ireland	1841	53
Italy	1871	64
Netherlands	1849	53
Norway	1891	57
Poland	1897	70
Portugal	1890	65
Spain	1860	72
Sweden	1860	67
Switzerland	1880	42
Russia	[1926]	82
[United States	1850	65]

Source: Bairoch, 1975, p.468.

France and Germany, had smaller percentages of their workforce engaged in agrarian occupations. Britain stands out as quite exceptional, though agriculture employed a quarter of the labour force. It's worth noting too the comparison with the United States, like Britain, France and Germany, a country experiencing industrialization, but where continuous westward expansion at least until the 1880s meant agriculture remained pre-eminent.

There are many caveats about such data: wide chronological differences between countries; questions of reliability; the danger of using concepts and classifications of modern society to describe traditional societies with a much greater overlap of economic activities, for example rural workers, engaged in textiles, coal mining, metal trades and other industrial occupations on a part-time basis, or communities in which there might be much under-employment seasonally.

In many of the states of Europe agriculture was one of the most important occupations. Certainly in the relatively backward periphery of Europe, as Pollard (1981, p.192) notes, agriculture provided the largest source of employment, and the single most important source of income and wealth, modest though that might have been. So the data in Table 1, in one sense, are a useful measure of comparative backwardness. At the other end of the economic spectrum the staying power of agriculture in Britain, as Anderson (pp.7–8) points out, is well illustrated by the fact that it was still the largest employer in 1851, and landed property represented 40 per cent of total capital – this in the most industrialized of the European states.

In some states of western Europe at the start of the nineteenth century the agricultural labour force had theoretically escaped from the bonds of feudalism, but this was far from universal, for serfdom was still legal in much of the centre and east. Admittedly the French Revolution had shaken élites everywhere and acted as the first major spur to reform, while the later revolutions of 1830 and 1848 had perhaps even greater immediate impact. While political considerations and fear of revolt were uppermost, there was also a growing recognition even among the most reactionary landlords, that new agricultural structures and methods might be more economic and pay higher profits than traditional serf-based production. Hence emancipation was an important development both politically and economically.

Exercise Read Anderson pp.106 and 191–2, and Document II.4, then answer the following questions.

1   Identify the main dates in the chronology of the emancipation laws for those countries mentioned by Anderson.

2   What are the key provisions of this decree (Document II.4) and what impact do you think they would have had on the peasants and land-owners? What strikes you about its date?

3   According to Anderson what were the effects of emancipation?

Specimen Answers 1   The chronology that can be constructed from the dates given by Anderson is potentially quite complex but looks roughly like this:

1780s	Habsburg Empire – First decree of Joseph II
1788	Denmark – Decree on emancipation
1807	Prussia – First decree
1808	Bavaria – First decree
1848	Austria – Edict of Ferdinand I
1850	Prussia – Decree abolishing remaining servile obligations
1861	Russia – Edict grants personal freedom to serfs
1864	Russian Poland – similar
1866–7	Similar for lands of Imperial family
1869	Cossack areas
1870	Transcaucasia

Note that there was often a considerable gap between the passage of the legislation and its implementation, seen in several states cited by Anderson, notably in Austria, Prussia, and Russia.

2   Servitude was abolished, as were all obligations to the lord on the part of the peasant. The land was to be freed of all burdens deriving from feudalism, but certain manorial rights were to be maintained, as seen under provision 7. Money compensation was to be paid for the relief of these burdens at rates to be set by a special commission

representing all the provinces of the state. Manorial authorities were to continue their administrative and political functions until the state was in a position to take over from them. The peasants would have to pay up for the relief of obligations brought by their freedom from slavery – hence greatly increasing the economic burdens of the peasant who might well lose out if certain rights, for example to grazing, were taken from him. Although the edict is not specific on the pro-noble implications, the lord probably stood to gain, assuming compensation levels were favourable – and he would be relieved of obligations to his former serfs who now became a peasant labour force, paid in the produce of their small land-holding and/or money wages.

The date coincides with the 1848 Revolutions, which had a considerable impact on Austria, and helped force political reforms such as this edict on emancipation. But note that while this was ostensibly a progressive piece of legislation, which was freeing the serfs, in reality it seems to favour the landowners, who were getting a fair bit from it.

3　There were long delays in the implementation of the emancipation laws and peasants were aggrieved about this and the cost of compensation paid to former lords. Communal disputes often dragged on for years. More generally emancipation had considerable impact in that it facilitated the modernization and commercialization of agriculture, assisted by improved transport, especially the railways, and by higher levels of literacy. Anderson (p.192) cites the example of Russia, where by 1914 more than three-quarters of the agricultural produce was marketed by peasants (often working communally), when at the date of emancipation in 1861 it had only been a tenth.

Edicts like the Austrian one raise the important question as to who was actually being liberated from communal obligation, the lords or the peasants, and in this and other similar enactments there is more than a suggestion, even a recognition, that serfdom was not as profitable as alternative agrarian systems. Like the profitability of slavery in the plantations of the southern United States before the Civil War, serfdom in eastern and central Europe raises some intriguing questions for the historian. Was serfdom profitable? If not why did it survive so long? Did it support the élite in non-economic ways, particularly in its status and political power within the state? Did emancipation have a greater impact than in Western Europe?

It is worth noting that in only one country where serfdom prevailed was the agrarian structure totally reshaped. In Denmark, where the subjugation of the peasantry had occurred as comparatively recently as the seventeenth century, the reforms did not merely involve liberation from servitude. The land-holdings were consolidated and enclosed (see below), credit was provided to enable the liberated peasants to buy the land they farmed, and in many cases to put up farm houses and buildings on the unified holdings. Within a few decades the Danish landscape was transformed and viable farms, in the hands of an independent peasantry capable of responding to further change, had been created (Anderson, p.191; Tracy, 1989, p.8).

Emancipation was obviously a major development in the history of agrarian structures during the nineteenth century, but did it make much difference to the lot of the peasant? Were the emancipated peasants of the central and eastern European states any better off than their western counterparts? To get an overview of the peasant's position we can turn again to Anderson.

Exercise   Read Anderson, pp.188–91. Draft an essay plan on the topic 'What was the general condition of the peasantry in nineteenth-century Europe and how was it changing?', and write a paragraph summarizing your approach.

Discussion   The first thing you might note, as Anderson himself does, is the danger of generalization. But since you have to begin somewhere, you could say that to the observer, peasant society in the nineteenth century remained very traditional and conservative, locked into old ways and beliefs, particularly about farming practice and religion, and generally resistant to change. But the peasantry was not a homogenous group: there were great differences in social and economic groupings, for example between the communal organization found in parts of Russia, and the individualistic approach prevalent in France. Peasants had a hard life and a standard of living inferior to townsfolk. They had a poor diet and were often exposed to shortages and even famine. They lived in primitive conditions and poor housing. Superstition and fear about these and other conditions were understandable looking at the list cited by Anderson (pp.190–1). But things were changing, particularly after the 1870s. According to Anderson emancipation had taken a long time to work its way through to the bulk of the peasantry of the east and centre, but was then having a greater impact on the status of the peasant, if not on his or her standard of living or short-term prospects. Another change was the exposure to modernization and particularly the market brought by better transport, education, and mass-produced goods – so that the peasant slowly began to acquire a better standard of living and new, mainly urban, values. Politically, as periodic demonstrations and revolts proved, the dissatisfied peasantry was potentially powerful and it slowly began to assert itself, by successful demands for change in its status and ultimately more democracy. Yet change was slow, with the peasantry characterized as inferior, inefficient in agricultural practices and conservative in outlook.

Something else that we could add from our earlier discussion on the role of demography in agricultural development is that much of agrarian Europe experienced sustained upturns in population during the nineteenth century which put pressure on cultivable land. In some places, like Ireland, Poland and Galicia, as Anderson (p.16) specifically highlights, this helped to create a landless peasantry, whose under- or unemployment forced seasonal then permanent migration in search of work.

Don't worry if you did not get all of this. Like the topic of agriculture itself you can see that this answer goes in a lot of different directions at once, and highlights the complex relationships between the changing agrarian structure and more general developments in the political and economic history of the major European states. But before we look at the political and economic dimensions let's briefly consider the role of new methods and technology in agricultural change during the nineteenth century.

Technology

As we have seen in our earlier discussion, agriculture occupied a large proportion of the workforce and throughout much of Europe was highly labour-intensive. This was certainly the case in the more backward regions on the periphery, but in the more advanced areas new methods of production, and particularly machinery, were of growing importance. Agriculture, mainly because of rising costs, was shedding labour and losing it as a result of migration to the towns and industry in many parts of Europe, so the initial impression one might have that mechanization was of little importance needs to be examined more critically.

What Bairoch (1975, p.460) calls 'the ways and means of the Agricultural Revolution' – six in all – can be summarized as follows:

1   gradual elimination of fallow land and its replacement by continuous rotation of crops;

2   introduction or extension of new crops;

3   improvement of traditional farm implements and introduction of new implements, particularly for harvesting;

4   selection of seed and breeding animals;

5   extension and improvement of arable land;

6   extension of the use of horses (and later steam engines and tractors) for farm work.

These developments assumed as a pre-condition the consolidation of holdings, as occurred in Denmark, for much of continental Europe was still cultivated on the strip system in open fields. A good example of early nineteenth-century reorganization, necessary before husbandry could be improved, comes from the village of Rempertshoven in Baden-Württemberg.

Exercise   Examine Figures 2 and 3. Note that areas in black all belong to one farmer. What changes are represented and what effects do you think resulted?

Discussion   Figure 2 shows the disparate nature of land use in the feudal agrarian structure. One farmer worked 35 or more strips scattered all over the village, which must have been very inefficient and allowed limited opportunities for improvement. In the aftermath of consolidation (Fig. 3) the same farmer worked three much larger holdings, which could be enclosed to facilitate the introduction of more efficient methods, new crops, and machinery. This suggests that with the creation of larger holdings many peasants lost out and either became labourers to the wealthier landowners or migrated to seek other employment, probably in industrial occupations.

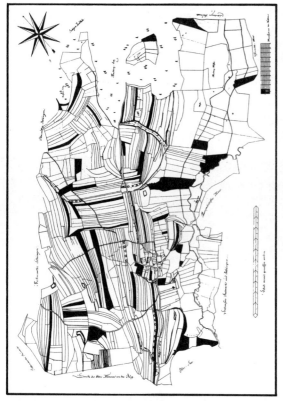

Figure 2
Rempertshoven, Baden-Württemberg, 1803 before consolidation. From Michael Tracy, Agriculture in Western Europe: Challenge and Response, 1880–1980, *2nd edn, London, Granada, 1982. Copyright: Landesamt für Flurbereinigung und Siedlung Baden-Württemberg.*

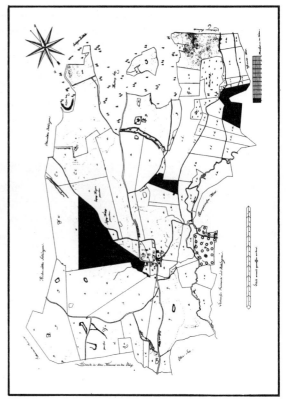

Figure 3
Rempertshoven, Baden-Württemberg, 1803 after consolidation. From Michael Tracy, Agriculture in Western Europe: Challenge and Response, 1880–1980, *2nd edn, London, Granada, 1982. Copyright: Landesamt für Flurbereinigung und Siedlung Baden-Württemberg.*

It is worth noting that this village had a total area of 252 ha, with 13 farmers cultivating an average of 20 ha each. There were 710 plots of roughly 0.35 ha each. This pattern was typical of conditions over a large part of western Europe. Rempertshoven was a fairly rare case of successful early consolidation. The number of plots was reduced to 36, averaging 7 ha each, with six farmsteads being moved out of the village. It was fortunate in that the agrarian structure did not seriously deteriorate again after this consolidation, and being in an area of mixed farming, survived the depression (see below) later in the century.

Apart from reorganization of land use the nineteenth century brought immense possibilities for technical improvements in agriculture. In Britain the age of 'High Farming' had arrived: soil was improved by drainage and fertilization; crop yields were increased; livestock breeds were improved;

new machinery was introduced and steam power became available for ploughing and threshing. Agricultural research progressed in Britain and later Germany, particularly in the field of soil chemistry and the use of artificial fertilizers. In the Netherlands and Belgium great progress was made in horticulture and fruit-growing, while Denmark pioneered factory-style dairying.

Where the new methods and machinery were applied they greatly enhanced productivity and the revolution in practice even percolated down from the improving landowners and big farmers to some of the smaller peasant farmers. We can catch some flavour of this in a description of French agriculture during the early 1880s.

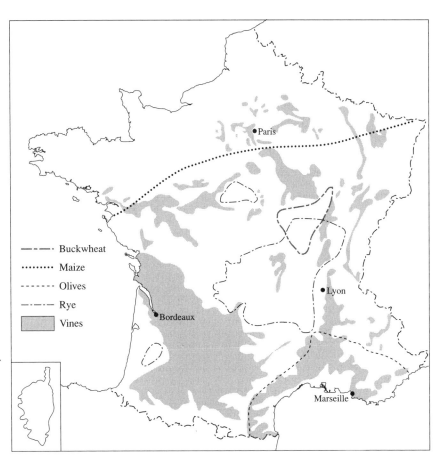

Figure 4
Agricultural geography of France, after Nicolet. From Hugh Clout, Agriculture in France on the Eve of the Railway Age, London, Croom Helm, 1980.

- — - — · Buckwheat
- ········· Maize
- - - - - - Olives
- - · — · - Rye
- ▨ Vines

Exercise   Examine Figure 4 and then read Document II.5 on agricultural progress in France, 1881. What does it tell us about agrarian structure in France, the main types of agriculture and products, the progress of new methods, and the use of machinery?

Discussion   The agriculture of France was rich and diverse, with a wide range of crops and generally high productivity. Most farmers, large and small, were very efficient, making use of fertilizers and machinery as appropriate. Broadly there were two types of farming found in France: *la petite culture* carried out on small, intensive farms; and *la grande culture* on larger more extensive holdings, the latter particularly common in Flanders.

According to the writer both had made great progress, though the traditional small-scale farms had adapted to a wide range of agricultural land use, arable and pastoral. Large areas of the south were devoted to the vine and olives and smaller areas to citrus fruits. Larger-scale farming concentrated on cereals, roots and sugar beet. Mechanization had made some progress, tending to become common on the larger farms, mainly because the terrain made machinery unsuitable for use on the smaller farms. Yet it had also made progress there and an interesting spin-off was the development of agricultural engineering and machinery hire by entrepreneurs.

Further confirmation of the progress of mechanization in French agriculture comes from Document II.6, where you can read of the enormous increase in the use of machinery that occurred between the 1860s and 1912, particularly of harvesting equipment like threshing machines and reapers. Please read Document II.6 now.

Note that petrol driven engines had already made their appearance. Mechanization, the author concludes, reduced costs and took the place of labour. Document II.6 thus accurately describes the state of agriculture in much of western Europe where great strides had been made during the nineteenth century. But we do have to remember that conditions in the more remote areas of France and indeed on much of the periphery, in Poland and Russia in the east, Spain and Italy in the south, were different and that agriculture was still little affected by new developments in technology.

Agriculture and economic growth

In this section we examine briefly the role of agriculture in the economic development of Europe during the nineteenth century. Let's look at what historians have written about the place of agriculture in the process of economic development which swept Europe in the period covered by this course.

Exercise   Read the following extracts then make your own summary of the various views presented. What major themes in the history of European agriculture do the four historians identify in these passages?

Extract 1

The term 'industrial revolution' denoting the period from the middle of the eighteenth century onwards, of gradual transition from traditionally agricultural societies to a type of economy in which industry was predominant, has often been criticized on the ground that the idea of 'revolution' conflicts with the idea of gradual transition. But the term is open to a much more justifiable objection, for the industrial revolution was really first and foremost an agricultural revolution which, in the societies where it occurred, permitted and fostered an unprecedented development of the industrial and mining sectors. The agricultural revolution – for so these profound changes in rural life have been rightly called – ended the deadlock, broke the stranglehold, and thus prepared the way for the industrial revolution.

As far as the agricultural revolution is concerned, though fresh research may still cause the generally accepted timing to be revised, it seems almost unthinkable that it can have begun much before the early eighteenth century.

Thus it can be stated with reasonable certainty that the agricultural revolution began in England about 1700, or at most a quarter of a century earlier. True, Kerridge's recent and well-documented study, unlike that of Chambers and Mingay, inclines to an even earlier date. The choice of the early eighteenth century does not, of course, exclude the possibility of progress or the introduction and application of certain new agricultural techniques in England even before that date; but it does mean that from that date onwards such progress was sufficiently widespread to exercise a perceptible influence on the English agricultural economy as a whole.

It is much more difficult to establish a chronology for the start of the agricultural revolution in other countries. Not only are there far fewer studies of the subject than in the case of England, but also the regional differences in most of the countries are much more marked. To say, for example, that the agricultural revolution reached Italy in 1820–30 could be quite misleading, given the present state of under-development of agriculture in large parts of the South and the high level already reached in the seventeenth century in the Po valley. In addition, the absence of political unity in many of the European countries before the mid-nineteenth century further complicates the question. For those reasons the dates given below must be taken as only approximate and subject to revision in the light of studies now being undertaken for most of those countries.

Approximate dates for the outset of the agricultural revolution in various countries are: England, 1690–1700; France, 1750–60; United States, 1760–70; Switzerland, 1780–90; Germany, Denmark, 1790–1800; Austria, Italy, Sweden, 1820–30; Russia, Spain, 1860–70.

For Belgium and the Netherlands it would be quite arbitrary to assign a date, for it was from Flanders and Brabant (the territories forming the Low Countries in the past) that the majority of the ideas originated on which the first stages of the agricultural revolution were based. (Bairoch, 1975, pp.452–60)

Extract 2

As a precondition for the industrialization of any society some reshaping of agrarian relations appears to be absolutely indispensable. The British case was exceptional because it took place so completely and apparently fitted in so well with the needs of an industrializing society. The same reasons which favoured the agrarian transition in England also prepared the conditions for industralization from a date much earlier than the eighteenth century. Agrarian change was in the main a response to what was going on outside agriculture, namely the growth of markets for food and industrial raw materials. It seems that it was the pressure of demand, and thus the possibilities of making profit by satisfying it, not anything happening in rural society, which prompted agrarian change. On the other hand, it is true that continued development of towns and the rise of markets would not have been possible had not a supply of raw materials and foodstuffs been made available. In that sense agrarian and industrial change, linked through the spread of market transactions and the development of the home market, acted in a close reciprocal relationship. If agrarian change was necessary for industrialization, then, it did not precede in time the preparation of the conditions, namely the extension of capitalist relations, but was an indispensable part of that process. Once it was under way changes in industry could stimulate technical improvement or reorganization in the agrarian sphere. At the same time, the introduction of new crops, the spread of technical skills or the availability of new aids to cultivation such as better tools and machines or artificial fertilizers, enabled agriculture to make a contribution of its own to economic growth. But there had to be a market for the increasing output, and some of these improvements required the attainment of a certain level of technical proficiency in industry or the expansion of trade, so the reciprocity is again established. (Kemp, 1985, pp.41–2)

Extract 3

A constantly recurring theme in our studies of economic development in western Europe has been the importance of the social changes brought about in the late eighteenth and early nineteenth centuries by the Enlightenment and the French Revolution. It was these changes which often enabled the smaller western European economies to respond so quickly to the rapid development of the larger economies in the nineteenth century. The most striking examples of this process are Denmark and Sweden which by 1914 had reached levels of per capita income almost as high as anywhere on the continent. The increased demand emanating from the major developed economies, the diffusion of technical knowledge and of capital, the increasing volume of intra-European trade and the specialization of function which this permitted, all seemed to suggest that, once the development of the larger economies was launched, the development of the rest of western Europe would inevitably follow provided no serious institutional obstacles stood in the way.

Two western European economies, however, Spain and Italy, which shared fully in the important institutional changes which began with the Enlightenment, and which were subject to the economic influence of the neighbouring developed economies, remained primarily agricultural economies until 1914. Their experience was not exactly parallel; after 1896 the growth of Italian industry distinguished it from the Spanish experience. In the last two decades of our period Italy began on a similar path of industrialization to that of the other western economies and by 1913 its per capita industrial output was comparable to that of Norway. Nevertheless by 1913 agriculture still contributed 37 per cent of gross domestic product and the industrial sector only 26 per cent. Agriculture still employed 58 per cent of the labour force and industry only 24 per cent. There are few statistical signposts through Spanish history and it is difficult to say anything about the composition and rate of growth of national income there. Estimates suggest that in 1914 some 38 per cent of national income still came from the agricultural sector and 26 per cent from mining and manufacturing. (Milward and Saul, 1977, pp.215–18)

Extract 4

Although we speak of feudal society and agrarian traditionalism, European agriculture, as far as we can tell, was never of one mould, and never entirely stable. Changes in population, in climatic conditions, in techniques and forms of organization, changes in markets and the political power of crown, nobility and gentry, kept the system in constant flux. By the later eighteenth century changes had become faster, and the differences between regions wider than ever.

It is not easy to impose order on the chaos of differing systems of tenure, of obligations, of payments, of technique, and of law which characterized European agriculture at the time. Nor is the task lightened by the fact that nowhere in economic life did legal or administrative fiction differ more widely from reality. For the land was difficult to supervise and control, and perhaps even to understand from the towns; customary relationships and unwritten conventions, in largely illiterate communities, were more significant than those rigidified on paper; and the exigencies or calamities of harvest failure, enemy occupation, epidemic, migration, or simple population rise could impose ad hoc solutions which could take a long time to find their way into the official or nominal structure.

One way of attempting to understand the reality of European agriculture is to begin with the recognition that, in addition to providing food and various raw materials, it had the purpose of providing large incomes for powerful classes in each society who offered little or no economic benefits in return. Human ingenuity and local historical conditions had built up a variety of rights, claims, obligations, or forms of ownership of land, all designed to transfer the largest possible share of income from the actual tiller of the soil to someone more powerful than he while leaving him just enough to carry on this process year after year. This transfer, according to circumstances, could be in the form of services, of payments in kind, or of cash, or of a mixture of them, the forms themselves, and the surrounding circumstances, being subject to significant changes, and carrying important implications. For our purposes, the most significant implication was the fact that important linkages existed between the form of agrarian tenure and preparedness for industrialization. (Pollard, 1981, pp.46–7)

Discussion   The key themes include:

1   the close relationship between agricultural change and industrialization;

2   the importance of social and demographic developments in forcing change;

3   the different timing in different countries;

4   the transitional nature of much of the change, particularly in those
     countries affected later rather than earlier;

5   the uneven effects of change, with large area of the periphery hardly
     touched by the modernisation of agriculture.

You should have picked out these (and perhaps other) points. It should not
have escaped your notice that each of these writers presents a slightly different interpretation of the links between agriculture and economic development, especially as regards timing. You should note the impetus
provided by developments in England, the Netherlands and Flanders to
early modernization, and the relative backwardness of peripheral states in
eastern and southern Europe. The linkages which existed between changes
in agrarian structure and early or 'proto' industrialization is also a common theme, emphasizing again the key role that agriculture can be seen to
have played in European economic growth before and during the nineteenth century.

'The Golden Age': landowners and agricultural policy to 1870

Even in the century of industrialization agriculture continued to underpin
the economy of many European states. Indeed, as Anderson (p.23) points
out, the creation of the state, at least in the case of German unification,
was as significant for the development of agriculture as it was for industry.
Unification abolished tolls on rivers and roads, led to the introduction of a
national currency and promoted greater trade in agricultural products as
well as manufactures. Occupying an important place in the economy, agricultural interests remained of considerable political significance, and it is
these and their relationship to the state that are briefly addressed now.

    Landowners continued to occupy an important, if in some states
declining, place in the political hierarchy. Again, as Anderson shows, there
were great differences to be found, particularly between the local and
national situations.

Exercise   Read Anderson, pp.184–7. Draft a paragraph summarizing how you would
tackle an essay with the title, 'What role did the landed class play in the
different states mentioned and how was this changing?'.

Discussion   As before there's no need to provide a model answer but the points you
should pick out from Anderson include the following.
    The land-owning class still had considerable clout in Britain,
Germany and Russia; its economic and social leadership allowing it to
exercise great political influence and control, especially at a local level. The

situation in Prussia and Russia, where the state actually made attempts to bolster the influence of the landed class to counter the march of liberal democracy inspired largely by the middle classes, might be usefully contrasted with that in France, where state appointed officials, the prefects, were the departmental representatives of central government, and after the revolution of 1830, rarely nobles. At national level the landed class also continued to exercise influence, though this varied in extent from state to state. Again the situation in Germany, where the political power of the landowners, was actually greater than it had been for a century, can be contrasted with that in Britain, where the landlord's power was in decline. The main reasons for the changing political status of the landed class were economic pressures, peasant demands, emancipation, democracy, and fiscal measures, particularly higher taxation. The position of the Junkers might be contrasted with that of the English aristocracy. Another development that needs to be mentioned is the changing character of the land-owning class, which began to be infiltrated by industrialists and high-ranking civil servants. One or more of these explanations for the changing nature of the landed class could be further developed in answering this question. The conclusion would be that the landed class was remarkably successful in maintaining its political position, but that it was losing out almost everywhere in varying degrees.

The Prussian land-owning class, the Junkers (briefly discussed by Anderson, p.186), offer an interesting case study in the remarkable staying power of the traditional European landed élite during the nineteenth century.

Exercise   Read Offprint 6 on the Junkers and then answer the following questions:

1   What impact did agrarian reform have on the Junkers' position?

2   What were the major threats to their status and power?

3   How were these countered and what was the long-term result?

4   What main points of comparison and contrast does Schissler draw between the Junkers and the English landed class?

Specimen Answers   1   The Junkers were able to turn the reforms to their own advantage, largely through the use of delaying tactics and compensation policies which worked in their favour. Nobles who had got themselves in debt benefited from moratoria on credit, and were also able to avoid taxation. Many peasants were unable to cope with the free market and therefore acquiesced in the lack of rights which emancipation might have abolished.

2   Increasing controls exercised by the state over their lands and labour; the erosion of noble privilege and infiltration of middle-class landowners; legal emancipation of the peasant labour force; and the transformation of peasant land into private property.

3   These were largely countered, until the 1870s, by the economic success of agriculture, first for the internal market and then for export. With the onset of depression caused by overseas competition,

especially from North America, the Junkers pressed for and obtained state aid in the form of protective tariffs. This further consolidated their economic position and allowed them to exercise considerable political power, seen, for example, in the Agrarian League. But protection was costly and Prussian agriculture became less and less competitive internationally.

4   There are some interesting points of comparison. Both based their wealth on the land and agriculture, dominated the army and government for much of the period, and were 'open' to outsiders like merchants, industrialists, lawyers, civil servants etc. Both were economically active and participated not only in agricultural modernization but also in industry and transport. But the Junkers were more aggressively conservative politically, the English landed gentry being generally responsive to reform in association with the middle class and within a well-established constitutional monarchy where parliament was sovereign.

The other side of the argument should be mentioned, for the Junkers, like their British counterparts, did slowly lose many of their privileged powers. The ability to promote free trade or gain protection was arguably not something confined to the Junkers, but a general capacity on the part of European farming interests to exercise considerable influence on political policy.

Agriculture was progressively added to the list of economic matters with which nineteenth-century states had to cope. Mid-century the latent strength of American agriculture had not yet made much impact, for the advance of technology had not reached the stage when American produce could be quickly and cheaply transported to Europe. Agricultural trade was still mainly intra-European and remained relatively unimportant in relation to production. Britain, as a result of its expanding urban, industrial population had already become a large net importer of food, but such imports, in spite of the repeal of the Corn Laws in 1846, were not a serious threat to British farming (Anderson, p.39). France imported some cereals, particularly wheat, and exported others. Germany imported grain for the consuming and livestock regions of the west, and exported wheat and rye from the great estates such as those of the Junkers in the east. Denmark at this time was also a net exporter, for livestock and dairying were yet to expand on any scale. Hungary was another major producer, traditionally feeding the rest of the Austro-Hungarian empire. The largest exporter of grain in the world was Russia.

In the free trade interlude that characterized the period from the late 1840s to the early 1870s trade between the states of Europe became more nearly free from tariffs and other restrictions than at any other time in the period under review. Britain took the lead, for the Free Trade movement (see Anderson, pp.231–3) had gathered momentum throughout the early part of the century and scored a spectacular breakthrough with the repeal of the Corn Laws in 1846. With its undisputed economic leadership Britain had everything to gain and little to lose from the greatest possible freedom of trade. Other states followed Britain's lead, though because industralization came later protection of their agriculture and manufactures was necessary to counter competition.

The most significant development came in 1860 with the signing of the Anglo-French Treaty of Commerce. Napoleon III, who in 1852 had established himself as emperor, with extensive powers, was favourably disposed to free trade and anxious for political reasons to establish close relations with Britain. There was considerable opposition in the French parliament but the treaty went ahead none the less. It was of significance not only for the reductions it made in French duties (and comparatively minor concessions by Britain), but also because it laid the basis for a series of subsequent treaties between France and other European states. Each was based on the 'most favoured nation' principle, so that the concessions granted to one state were automatically extended to the others. Thus throughout most of Europe trade was freed or subject only to low duties (Anderson, pp.231–2).

Because it was in the best interests of most states, the trade in primary products became even freer than that in manufactures. By 1860 Britain had abolished duties not only on cereals but on almost all other farm imports, leaving only a few revenue duties. France practically removed agricultural protection in the 1860 treaty and a year later abolished related cereal duties. German producers, heavily reliant on exports, also favoured free trade: cereal duties had been abolished by the Zollverein in 1853. In Italy moderate Piedmontese duties formed the basis of the tariff for the unified kingdom, and after treaties with France and other states, agriculture was protected with only low duties on cereals. The Netherlands dropped cereal duties in 1862 and Belgium followed in 1871. Primary products could move freely from state to state as the market demanded, a situation which brought benefits both to producers and consumers. Economic competition between the states of Europe, if not suspended, was for a period temporarily shelved.

You should now read Anderson, pp.230–3 to set this specific discussion of agricultural trade in the general context of European free trade before the 1870s.

Foreign competition, depression and adjustment after 1870

After 1870 European agriculture was increasingly exposed to competition from primary products imported from areas of recent settlement in North America, South America, Australasia and elsewhere. Moreover the expansion of cereal production also brought cheaper grain from eastern Europe and Russia. This was made possible by the opening up of virgin lands and facilitated by cheaper transport. In North America particularly, the availability of vast land resources coupled with increased mechanization brought extremely cheap production. Russia's main advantages lay in plenty of land and cheap labour. In the 1850s American railroads began to penetrate the west and by the early 1880s the Rockies could be reached by seven different lines in the United States and Canada. In Russia new railways brought grain to ports on the Baltic and Black Seas. At the same time ships increased greatly in size and carrying capacity; sail gave way to steam, and the compound engine, which greatly reduced fuel costs, was adopted from the 1860s.

As Pollard (1981, p.266) observes data on wheat output, freight rates and exports are useful in showing the scale of North American expansion and its impact on Europe. Wheat production rose everywhere that extensive production was environmentally feasible. The resulting influx of cheap grain had a huge impact on European agriculture.

Table 2: Freight rates and prices for wheat

	Freight rates (pence per quarter)		Price of US wheat from Atlantic ports, c.i.f. Liverpool (pence per quarter)
	Chicago to New York, by railroad	New York to Liverpool, by steamer	
1870–74	113	66	625*
1875–9	72	60	568*
1880–84	63	35	531
1885–9	61	25	402
1890–94	53	20	379
1895–9	47	23	356

* Including wheat from Pacific ports from 1871 through 1875.

Source: Board of Trade (1903), cited in Tracy, 1989, p.17.

Table 3: Exports of wheat

	USA	Canada	Russia *million bushels*	India	Australasia
1851–60	5	-	41	-	-
1861–70	22	-	75	-	-
1870–74	59	1	55	1	-
1875–79	107	3	71	6	-
1880–84	136	4	65	29	-
1885–89	110	3	95	36	-
1890–94*	170	9	104	30	8
1895–99*	184	16	107	15	3

* Data include wheat flour (in wheat equivalent) – the amounts involved, however, are relatively small.

Source: Tracy, 1989, p.18.

Exercise   Examine Tables 2 and 3 (above), and comment on what the data show.

Discussion   Table 2 shows the extent of the fall in transport costs from the 1870s to the 1890s, when the cost of railroad and shipping was cut by a half in the first decade and nearly a third over the whole period. The price of American wheat arriving in Liverpool fell by even more than the amount of the reduction in transport costs. Wheat exports from the United States rose sharply in the 1870s and kept rising until the mid-1880s, when there was a temporary fall. Exports from Russia also grew rapidly over the period.

Canada was beginning to make an impact on the world market, while the opening of the Suez Canal in 1869 promoted faster trade with India and Australia. Meantime grain prices fell steadily.

These developments had severe implications for European cereal producers, especially in the west, with general economic depression and falling prices prevailing throughout the years 1873–1896, which came to be characterized as the 'Great Depression'. In its early stages the crisis mainly affected cereals but, with the development of refrigeration, chilled then frozen meat reached Europe from the United States in 1879 and from Australia in 1880, and shipments grew enormously from then on. However the production of livestock products, including dairy products, was rising less rapidly than cereals, while with the gradual improvement of the standard of living the demand for livestock products was increasing comparatively fast. Thus the fall in prices of livestock and related products was never as great as that of cereals. The British experience was fairly typical: the price of livestock products did not fall until 1885, at least five years after the major fall for cereals occurred, and at the trough of the depression in 1896, livestock prices were 75 per cent of their pre-depression level when arable prices were 50 per cent.

This difference in the trend of prices, as Tracy (1989, pp.18–19) points out, was of considerable significance. It meant that the effects of the depression were not felt equally by cereal and arable farmers. The former suffered directly from the reduced value of their produce, while the latter also suffered a fall in value, but it came later and was not so serious. And livestock farmers actually benefited from the much greater fall in the price of feed grains. The impact was partly geographical, on the large grain growing areas of East Prussia, Flanders and East Anglia, for example, and partly related to the scale of farming carried on in particular regions. Cereal farming tended to be extensive on large farms and estates, whereas smaller farms – including peasant holdings – were more likely to be devoted to arable or mixed agriculture with dairy cows, pigs, poultry, and cereal or other fodder crops. Again these differences are important for understanding the agricultural depression. The farmers best able to influence government policy were the larger farmers, often the landed class, for the peasants were generally unorganized and unrepresented. This suggests that the traditional view of the 'Great Depression' may have exaggerated its severity. Too much emphasis was put on the fall in cereal prices and the unfavourable consequences for arable farmers. Not enough attention was paid to the much less difficult situation of livestock producers. When various European states introduced protection they did so largely at the instigation of the larger producers and for their benefit. For the peasantry the advantages of protection were much less evident.

Exercise You should now read Document II.7 (a) and (b) which confirms the impact of competition and its severe effects on western Europe. What factors contributed to the flood of cheap grain from North America, and what other sources of imports are mentioned? What results are indicated by the authors?

Discussion   Extract (a) emphasizes first, the significance of cheaper shipping despite
the enormous distances involved; and secondly, a huge expansion of
cereal cultivation in the American West. Extract (b) highlights the
immediate impact of the depression with huge falls in prices of cereals
caused by the flood of produce from eastern Europe, North America,
India and Argentina. Consequently agricultural rents and land values fell
and there was growing indebtedness among farmers, including peasant
holdings.

All of this suggests that the best policy for European agriculture during the 'Great Depression' was a shift from crop production to livestock
and livestock products. States which were far-sighted enough to do this and
had a more mixed agriculture in the first place stood a much better chance
of overcoming the crisis than those which in the face of the new trends,
persevered with existing practices.

As Kemp (1985, p.47) indicates, specialization and production for the
changing market became increasingly important and points to the case of
Denmark. Here specialization on livestock and dairy products in a new
'industrialized' agriculture coupled with the development of co-operatives
literally saved the bacon of Danish producers. The Danes went for 'value
added' products and their example was followed elsewhere, notably in
the Netherlands, Switzerland, Italy and in a minor way in Britain. Document II.8 (a) gives some indication of how progressive the Danish model
was, while II.8 (b) describes the development and operation of farm co-
operatives in Italy before the First World War. You should read these
now.

Figure 5
The first co-operative
dairy in Denmark. (From:
J.W. Murray, Growth and
Change in Danish
Agriculture, *Hutchinson*
Benham, 1977, Federation
of Danish Co-operative
Societies.)

Most of the developed countries were greatly alarmed by the exposure to foreign competition and paid a great deal more attention to the importance of agriculture, the need for improved efficiency, and greater research on soils, crops and animals. In Britain there were detailed parliamentary commissions into the state of agriculture and the impact of the depression, which revealed the fact that the cereal producing districts of southern and eastern England had been worst hit, while the areas of more mixed or purely livestock production were not quite so badly off. In France there was belated recognition that the state needed to be more interventionist, hence the establishment in 1881 of a new, separate, Ministry of Agriculture. This is explained in Document II.9 which you should read now.

Exercise Having read Document II.9 try to explain why did Gambetta urge the establishment of the ministry?

Discussion Agriculture was central to the French economy, and reform was urgent given foreign competition, the depression, poor harvests and the drastic effects of phylloxera, which had devastated French vineyards. Resources needed to be devoted to education, research, inspection and incentives to encourage new methods.

However, the common reaction of European governments to the blast of overseas competition was a return to protection after the free trade interlude initiated in 1860. Nationalist sentiment played a part in this, particularly in France and Germany in the aftermath of the Franco-Prussian War of 1870. Another important factor was the increasing concern with industrial development for demands from industrialists became more insistent, showing that they had never really been converted to free trade. Public opinion also played a part because the depression hit wages and profits and reduced purchasing power. The protectionist movement, particularly in Germany, drew inspiration from the school of nationalist economics, with its stress on economic development through protection. There and elsewhere there was ample scope for powerful protectionist alliances between agricultural and industrial interests. The reversal of policy was marked progressively with the introduction of agricultural tariffs in Italy in 1878, Germany in 1879, and France in 1881, with other states following in their footsteps during the 1880s. In the United States developing industries were protected and this was extended, under the McKinley Tariff of 1890, to agriculture. In most countries which adopted protection for agriculture the degree of protection before the First World War was between 20 and 30 per cent.

There were important exceptions, notably Britain, which stuck to free trade despite overseas competition. A large sector of British agriculture, as Tracy (1989, p.23) notes, was effectively ruined, 'High Farming' giving way to the utmost economy and initiating further large-scale drift from the countryside.

Surprisingly there was no really effective move for protection among the farmers themselves and only after the end of the depression, from 1903–5, did a vigorous campaign for tariff reform begin. This was based on a desire to secure preferences for Empire trade rather than simply the protection of British agriculture and the conflict between the two was never satisfactorily reconciled. The successful campaign against the Corn Laws had left a deeply ingrained hostility to any tax on foodstuffs for 'cheap bread' remained a powerful rallying cry.

Several factors outside agriculture influenced the policies individual states adopted. These included economic theory, strategic interests and public opinion, and all three affected the nature of alliances between agricultural and industrial interests in different countries. Conflict between the two sectors was probably always inevitable, because protection for industry was likely to raise the cost of farm equipment and wages. Protection for agriculture, by raising food prices, increased labour and raw material costs. The latter was not particularly serious since many industrial materials, for example, cotton were produced overseas, but wool was an important exception and the result of competition from Australia, South America and elsewhere was a fall in sheep numbers all over Europe. Conflict was also inevitable when industry sought to enlarge its export markets. In Germany this problem became acute in the 1890s, and the fact that it was resolved in favour of agriculture demonstrated the political strength of the farmers.

The influence of the agricultural community was largely a reflection of the relative size of the agricultural population. It was also determined by the extent to which democracy had eroded the political power of the landed class.

In Britain, as we saw, political reforms starting with the first Reform Act had weakened the power of the landed élite, and probably as important, divisions between landlord and tenant, and between cereal and livestock farmers prevented the formation of any coherent agricultural pressure group. In both Denmark and the Netherlands significant reforms had created independent and energetic farmers, who through adaptation and greater efficiency were able to rise to the challenge of new conditions. But in states with a dominant class of large landowners (interested primarily in the price of cereals), this group was able to present itself as representative of the whole agricultural interest, regardless of the real needs of other sectors, and to exert great influence on government policy. So in Germany the Junkers, again as we noted, remained a coherent group with vestiges of feudal power and an entrenched position in the state, active in the Agrarian League (see Anderson, p.316), which kept rural interests at the forefront of politics in this period. In France the campaign for protection was led by the aristocratic *Societé des Agriculteurs de France*, and in Italy by the big grain producers.

The challenge of foreign competition produced different responses. In many states, particularly France and Germany, there was a defensive reaction, with greatly increased tariff protection so that farmers were shielded from the worst effects of the depression, partly by an expanding rather than a static home market, but the incentive to adjust was probably diminished. Britain maintained free trade and so adjustment forced the decline of the arable sector – at considerable economic and social costs. Later the larger farms achieved comparatively high labour productivity and incomes. In Denmark and the Netherlands the response was positive, protection was eschewed and adaptation brought improved farm production and marketing, to the benefit of the economy as a whole. To a large extent the different reactions were determined by earlier social, political and economic developments. In France, Germany and to a lesser extent Russia, while the mass of the peasantry remained backward, the large farmers and landowners still had political influence and were able to join forces with industrialists to fight for protection – even in the German case, to prevail over manufacturing when interests diverged. In Britain the urban population and industrial interest were already economically and politically predominant.

If the protectionist response was thus largely predetermined, it was not inevitable that the states which followed this road should have pursued so little positive adjustment. It would have been possible, while supporting farm prices through tariffs, to encourage technical progress, consolidate holdings, promote more intensive agriculture and develop rural industries. But in reality protectionist attitudes inhibited such developments and adjustment being made less urgent was constantly deferred. The legacy, as Tracy (1989, p.32) wrote, extended far beyond 1914. It's worth noting, however, that some historians have disputed the general economic significance of agricultural tariffs and the claim that industry was sacrificed to agriculture.

Conclusion

In concluding your work on this unit you should look back at the aims set and think about answers of the kind that might form the basis of a response to an essay question on each topic set out in the aims. You could see this as a final exercise for this unit.

I will not provide answers but suggest you look back over the unit and associated reading if the key issues are not immediately clear to you. This discussion of the role of agriculture in economic development leads naturally to your work in Unit 9 on industrialization in nineteenth-century Europe, another key process in the rise of the major nation states before 1914.

References

Aldcroft D.H and Ville, S.P. (1994), *The European Economy 1750–1914: A thematic Approach*, Manchester University Press, Manchester.

Bairoch, P. (1975), 'Agriculture and the Industrial Revolution 1700–1914' in C.M. Cipolla (ed.), *The Fontana Economic History of Europe. The Industrial Revolution*, 2nd edn, Fontana-Collins, London.

Clout, H. (1980), *Agriculture in France on the Eve of the Railway Age*, Croom Helm, London.

Deane, P. (1975), *The First Industrial Revolution*, Cambridge University Press, Cambridge.

Kemp, T. (1985), *Industrialization in Nineteenth-Century Europe*, 2nd edn, Longman, London.

Lieven, D. (1992), *The Aristocracy in Europe 1815–1914*, Macmillan, London.

Milward, A.S. and Saul, S.B. (1977), *The Development of the Economics of Continental Europe 1850–1914*, Allen & Unwin, London.

Mitchell, B.R (1981), *European Historical Statistics*, 2nd revised edn, Macmillan, London.

Moeller, R.G. (ed.) (1986), *Peasants and Lords in Modern Germany. Recent Studies in Agricultural History.* Allen & Unwin, Boston.

Pollard, S. (1981), *Peaceful Conquest. The Industrialization of Europe 1760–1970*, Oxford University Press, Oxford.

Post, J.D. (1977), *The Last Great Subsistence Crisis in the Western World*, Johns Hopkins University Press, Baltimore and London.

Tracy, M. (1989), *Government and Agriculture in Western Europe 1880–1988*, Harvester Wheatsheaf, London.

Webb, S. (1982), 'Agricultural Protection in Wilhelminian Germany: forging an empire with pork and rye', *Journal of Economic History*, 42, pp.309–26.

Unit 9
Patterns of European industrialization

Prepared for the course team by Bernard Waites

Contents

Study timetable

Weeks of study	Texts	Video	AC
3	Unit 9; Anderson	Video 2 (Section 4 by Michelle Perrot; Sections 5–10 by Clive Trebilcock and Sidney Pollard)	

Before starting this unit you should have read these sections of Anderson: pp.6–11 (analysing the economic strength of the major European powers *c*.1815); pp.29–32 (comparing the British and German economies in the late nineteenth-century); pp.125–55 (a more extended analysis of industrial growth and the transport revolution). You have already encountered key concepts in the study of industrialization from the discussion on Video 2 by Sidney Pollard and Clive Trebilcock, viewed in connection with the Block Introduction. At certain points, I will suggest a re-viewing of specified passages.

Aims
The aims of this unit are to address the following questions:

1   How did the different European powers come to be industrialized?

2   What 'routes' did they follow in the transition to modern society?

3   What measures did states take to overcome their self-perceived 'backwardness'?

4   Why was Britain displaced as the leading industrial power by Germany after about 1890?

After analysing the industrialization process synoptically, and emphasizing its regional dimension, we will turn to a more detailed discussion of France, Germany and Russia. Britain will be discussed solely in terms of the applicability of otherwise of Rostow's 'stage theory' of economic growth.

Introduction

Industrialization brought a fundamental discontinuity in the rate of economic change in human history. Had the British economy continued to grow after 1750 at the same rate as during the previous half century, it would have taken national income 120 years and per capita income as long as 346 years to double in size. By the second quarter of the nineteenth century national income could be predicted to double every 28 years and per capita income every 63 years (O'Brien, 1993, p.9).

Explaining *why* modern industrial growth began in north-west Europe, and in England rather than France, would take us beyond the confines of this course. But we must not begin by assuming that pre-industrial economies were tradition-bound and static. Indeed, there are powerful arguments for viewing industrialization as the sequel to a cumulative process of technical and institutional improvements – dating back to the Middle Ages – by which Europe slowly enhanced its natural advantages over other major cultural areas. Key institutional advances before 1700 were the securing of individual property rights against arbitrary violation by the state, and the emergence of legal devices (such as the joint-stock company) for spreading economic risk. In early nineteenth-century Europe, the economic potential of an endowment of medieval techniques was still far from exhausted. The motive power for most of the growth in output before 1850 came from the water-wheel: of 100,163 French industrial concerns surveyed between 1861–5, 60 per cent were water-powered and only 31 per cent steam-powered (Lévy-Leboyer, 1978, p.267). The falling price of an English pocket watch – a complex consumer durable – from about £20 to £1 in the century *before* 1776, testifies to the routinization of precision skills and the growth of a large market for what in other regions of the world were the playthings of despots.

Defining industrialization

Technological change

Before continuing with the unit you should look again at Video 2, Section 5, pp.610–747.

Industrialization can be defined in two, analytically distinct ways: the first is in terms of a generalized process of *technological innovation* involving the substitution of inanimate power for human and animal effort, the mechanization of handicrafts, and the displacement of manual skills by machine operations. The best-known innovations are associated with specific inventions (such as Matthew Boulton's development of James Watt's separate condenser into an economically viable steam engine), but invention is not a sufficient condition for innovation. Innovation requires entrepreneurs to make a sustained and costly effort to exploit technical improvements. Several periods in European medieval and early modern history have been identified with bursts of technological innovation, but it is generally agreed that later eighteenth-century Britain witnessed a unique burst of technological innovation that raised the annual growth of the economy to unprecedented levels. Previous phases of European growth had petered out when confronted by the natural check of the diminishing rate

Time chart of the technological innovations of the 'First Industrial Revolution'

1709	Darby produces first coke-smelted iron
1712	Newcomen develops first commercially viable steam pump
1733	Kay's flying shuttle roughly doubles weaver's output (in widespread use by 1755)
1740s	advances in production of sulphuric acid (an industrial bleach)
c.1750	coke-smelting leads to wider use of cast-iron
c.1764	Watt devises the separate condenser for the steam engine
1768	Hargreaves spinning jenny allows one spinner to work many (eventually 100+) spindles
1769	Arkwright's 'water frame' permits application of water-power to spinning
c.1770	radical improvements in Newcomen engine raises capacity to 70 HP
1776	first installation of a Watt steam engine to power bellows in iron-smelting
1779	construction of Severn iron bridge
1779	Crompton's mule takes mechanized spinning a stage further
1781→	Watt engine adapted to rotative powering of machinery
1784	Cort perfected puddling process to convert pig iron to wrought iron
c.1787	adoption of chlorine bleaching process
c.1790–1800	breakthrough in the spinning mule's adaptation to power-driven factory machine
1793	Eli Whitney's cotton gin facilitates separation of cotton fibre from seed and lowers raw cotton prices
c.1798	invention of bleaching powder overcomes bleaching bottleneck in textiles
1801	first viable steam ship constructed
1804	Trevithick demonstrates the first steam locomotive
c.1820	400 miles of iron track around Newcastle provides easy-running surface for horse-drawn wagons
c.1822	Richard Roberts achieves 'breakthrough' in design of power looms
c.1825	beginnings of large-scale alkali manufacture utilizing Leblanc process → origins of modern chemicals industry
1825	Stockton-Darlington railway opens
1825–30	Roberts develops fully self-acting mule as a power-driven machine no longer requiring skilled attention
1827	Marc Séguin develops the tubular boiler that improves steam engine efficiency
1830	first true public railway links Liverpool-Manchester
1830 →	development of continuous production in paper-making
1832	Benoit Fourneyron patents hydraulic turbine → encourages industrial application of water power in France and Switzerland
1837	first practical telegraph installed
1838	first continuous steam crossing of the Atlantic
1850	by now, 6,000 miles of railway laid in Britain
1856	introduction of the Bessemer process for converting pig iron into steel

Source: Lilley, 1973

of returns from agricultural expansion into less fertile soils (and the resulting disparity between population increase and declining food resources). Economic growth in later eighteenth-century Britain proved to be self-sustaining, and has continued (albeit unevenly) to this day. We call this innovative burst *the (first) Industrial Revolution*, and it was further unprecedented in the way its innovatory techniques and practices diffused outward from a single centre, first to Continental Europe and North America, later to the wider world.

The data in Table 1 give a fair measure of the progress of cotton industrialization and the increases in iron output that resulted from the coke-fuelled blast furnace; they show the 'early start' and enormous preponderance of British mechanized industry before 1870.

Table 1: Indicators of early industrialization

	Britain	Belgium	France	Germany	Russia
Raw cotton consumption (000s metric tons)					
1801	24	-	-	-	-
1811	40	-	-	-	1.4
1821	59	2.0	-	-	1.0
1831	119	1.0	28	2.4	1.7
1841	199	7.6	56	11.1	5.1
1851	299	10.0	58	17.1	23.0
Cotton spindles (000s)					
1834	10,000	200	2,500	626	700
1852	20,977	400	4,500	900	-
1861	30,387	612	5,500	2,235	1,000
Pig-iron output (000s metric tons)					
1800	160	-	-	-	180
1819	280	-	113	-	132
1825	580	-	199	95	158
1835	930	115	295	155	175
1850	2,250	145	406	210	228
Steam power capacity (000 HP)					
1850	1,290	70	370	260	-
1869	4,040	350	1,850	2,480	-

Source: Mitchell, 1992, pp.446–7, 490, 496–7, except steam power for which see Landes, 1969, p.194.

Historians commonly identify a 'Second Industrial Revolution' with a cluster of innovations whose systematic exploitation began about 1890, though their origins lay in earlier decades: electrical power and motors; organic chemistry and synthetics; the internal combustion engine and automotive devices; precision manufacture and assembly-line production (Landes, 1969, p.235; Anderson, p.128). The term 'revolution' implies a radical break with the past, and with respect to technique there was. Many of these innovations were derived from scientific research (rather than the practical 'know how' of earlier industrialization) and the 'Second Industrial Revolution' can be seen as the enlistment of basic science into the productive forces of modern societies. Whether there was such a 'break' in economically measurable terms (such as the increase in industrial output per head) is much more debatable. The issue hinges on whether we see economic growth as discontinuous (with a period of stagnation in the leading economies during the so-called 'Great Depression' of *c*.1873–93), or essentially continuous with a mere slackening after the early 1870s affecting primarily the early industrializers. The economic indices mostly discount the once commonly held view of European industrial capitalism gripped by a prolonged crisis. Despite the financial disasters of 1873–5, when companies were liquidated all over the world, manufacturing output grew substantially in the major European economies during the 1870s. (The indices in Table 5, below, will confirm this for you.) The 'Great Depression' was essentially a crisis of adjustment for Europe's peasantry to the new international division of labour created by the transport revolution and the unbeatable competition of prairie farmers. In manufacturing, the 'Second Industrial Revolution' was not a new beginning, but an intensification of processes rooted in the earlier phase of industrialization.

Structural change

Our second definition of industrialization starts not with technology but with the division of the labour force between the major *sectors* of the economy and involves a major shift in the distribution of the labour force from the primary to the secondary sector, or in other words a decline in the *proportion* of workers in agriculture and increase of that in manufacturing. This occupational shift results in a rise in manufacturing's contribution to GNP. Where and when such a shift occurred in Europe after about 1830, the increase in sectoral output was always greater than the rise in manufacturing's 'share' of the occupational structure because productivity gains in manufacturing were larger. For, among other things, more *capital*, in the form of tools, machines and buildings, was *invested* per worker in manufacturing. Not only were higher productivity techniques more available in industry than agriculture throughout most of the nineteenth century, market demand for industrial products was more resilient than for food and agricultural raw materials.

Proto-industrialization: structural change without technological innovation

It might reasonably be objected that, in empirical terms, our two definitions amount to the same thing: technological innovation – you could argue – necessarily entails a structural shift in the labour force, and the composition of the labour force is determined by the level of technique achieved by a society's productive apparatus. In the very long run of human history, these assertions may be true, but in the period covered by this course they cannot be accepted without major qualification. A widespread structural shift towards manufacturing occurred in later eighteenth- and early nineteenth-century Europe without the adoption of the technological innovations we associate with the Industrial Revolution. Much of the growth in output of textiles in Flanders and Silesia, of clocks in the Black Forest and Switzerland, of gloves around Grenoble resulted from a system of rural manufacturing using traditional implements and what was in effect surplus labour during slack periods of the agricultural year. The system has been called *proto-industrialization*, rather misleadingly perhaps since it was not a 'model' or prototype for industrialization based on innovative technology, and the areas where the system flourished did not necessarily develop into Europe's industrial regions.

Proto-industrial production for the market was organized by merchant capitalists who 'put out' materials to be worked up in the rural household, often by women, for piece wages. Frequently, this decentralized production was linked to a 'manufactory' where the finishing processes (such as fulling and dyeing) went on under one roof. Entrepreneurs were thus able to bypass the high labour costs and restrictive practices of the towns, and supply cheap manufactures to increasingly distant markets. Comparative research has shown a tendency for this type of manufacturing employment to have been concentrated in inherently infertile regions where agricultural earnings were low. Grain and other foodstuffs were 'imported' in exchange for manufactured 'exports'. It has been found that when the prices of manufactures were high and of food low, early marriage led to rapid population growth in proto-industrial regions. (An example is the textile region of Eastern Flanders where before the 1840s one worker in three depended more on linen than on farming for his/her bread.) But these relatively dense populations of household producers were desperately exposed when the last great subsistence crisis hit western Europe in 1846. The Flemish linen industry contracted and mechanized in response to the crisis, leaving domestic spinners and weavers to subsist on tiny holdings amidst poverty and hunger matched only in Ireland. The reversal of fortune during the nineteenth century for what had been one of the richest and most developed areas of Continental Europe was tragic and complete (Milward and Saul, 1973, p.448).

However, what is more remarkable is the persistence of rural household production in the Rhineland, Westphalia and other proto-industrial regions long after the first Lancashire-style textile factories had been erected in western Prussia during the 1830s. Before mid-century, writes Trebilcock (1981, p.35), 'the modern scale-intensive organizations worked much less to replace the proliferating craft system than to replace British imports'. Small units of low capital intensity and basic technology provided the major part of German textile output up to about 1850. Machine-spinning of linen yarn did not definitely replace hand-spun output until 1870, and the mechanization of weaving followed even more slowly. As late as 1882, one-third of all German textile workers still worked within the domestic system of production. Furthermore, there was a strong continuity between the capital and expertise accumulated in the Rhenish putting-out and manufactory enterprises and industrialization proper; in the skilled textile, paper and metal trades of Düren, for example, putting-out and manufactory masters retained their position in the local economy by introducing machinery and a more specialized division of labour under the spur of competition (Trebilcock, 1981, p.38, p.45; Kocka, 1978, p.508).

Different rates of structural change in Europe

Not only did structural change often take place without prior technical innovation, major European economies (such as France) adopted modern manufacturing techniques in certain industries, and achieved huge increases in
output, but in 1901 retained a proportion of their labour force in agriculture
equal to, or greater than, Britain's in 1801. We could say that in such cases
structural change tended to 'lag behind' the Industrial Revolution.

Table 2: Sectoral shares of GNP

	Agriculture	Manufacturing	Services	
Austria-Hungary(1911–1913)	49.0	38.0		13.0
Belgium (1910)	8.9	45.9		45.2
Denmark (1910)	30.0		M & S	70.0
France (1908–10)	35.0	37.0		28.0
Germany (1910–13)	23.4	44.6		32.0
Italy (1913)	37.0	26.0		39.0
Netherlands (1913)	16.3	26.7		57.0
Norway (1910)	24.0	26.0		50.0
United Kingdom (1907)	7.0	43.0		50.0
Russia (1913)	47.7	21.7		–

Source: Milward and Saul, 1977, p.517, except Russia where the figures come from Shanin,
1985, p.112.

Exercise   Space is too limited to provide a conventional narrative of European industrialization and in this exercise I want you to think synoptically about the
early twentieth-century 'end' of the story. Which were the most
'industrialized' economies by that date? One measure of industrialization
would be in terms of the *output* of manufacturing as a proportion of
national product, and Table 2 shows the share of different sectors in various countries in the early twentieth century. In which economies had
industrialization gone furthest? Do the data suggest different 'patterns' of
development?

Discussion   If we correlate industrialization with the decline of agriculture's share in
total output, then the process was clearly most advanced in Britain and
Belgium. Manufacturing was proportionally most important in Belgium,
closely followed by Germany. What you may find surprising is that Britain
belonged to a cluster of economies in which *services* were the most important sector, though the Netherlands was the most specialized of the 'service
economies'. Amongst the western economies, there is a clear difference in
'patterning' between Britain and Belgium on the one hand, and France
and Germany on the other. As we will discuss below, Germany's industrial
economy was easily the biggest in Europe in terms of total output, yet agriculture still accounted for a quarter of gross national product (GNP). In
France, agricultural and industrial output were approximately equal.
Finally, you will have noted that though the Habsburg and Tsarist Empires
were still overwhelmingly agrarian in terms of their social structure, agriculture accounted for slightly less than half of total output.

Table 3: Distribution of the economically active population in selected European countries (000s)

	I	II	III	IV	V	VI	VII	VIII
Belgium								
Males:								
1856	712	63	400	62	53	126	132	-
1910	585	192	807	185	182	184	256	-
Females:								
1856	354	10	317	-	32	1	115	-
1910	217	8	383	2	111	7	342	-
France								
Males:								
1856	5,146	177	2,002	486	510	214	1,174	-
1906	5,525	279	3,169	539	972	631	1,913	-
Females:								
1856	2,159	17	1,095	16	228	10	889	-
1906	3,330	6	2,059	1	642	241	1,422	-
Germany								
Males:								
1882	5,702	569	3,721	940	678	423	1,173	168
1907	5,284	1,197	5,959	1,887	1,251	983	1,907	114
Females:								
1882	2,535	22	995	6	176	14	443	67
1908	4,599	48	1,875	19	549	43	1,069	42
Russia								
Males:								
1897	15,077	155	2,920	671	1,051	649	3,207	227
Females:								
1897	1,867	8	894	2	141	21	1,777	-
Britain								
Males:								
1851	1,824	383	2,349	496	91	433	482	438
1911	1,489	1,202	4,688	1,140	739	1,571	1,361	741
Females:								
1851	230	11	1,263	1	-	13	1,241	75
1911	117	8	2,430	5	157	38	2,560	98

Key
I=Agriculture, Forestry and Fishing,
II=Extractive Industry,
III=Manufacturing Industry,
IV=Construction
V=Commerce and Finance,
VI=Transport and Communications,
VII=Services,
VIII=Others Occupied

Source: Mitchell, 1992, pp.142–56.

Exercise   Now I want you to compare the distribution of the economically active population in various European countries at different points in time in order to get a more 'social' sense of the impact of industrialization. Please refer to Table 3. Where was the majority of the male labour force to be found in manufacturing and mining? Which national economy made proportionally greatest use of women's labour outside the home? Why?

Discussion   *Nowhere in Europe* was a majority of the male labour force found in manufacturing and mining before 1911. This sector employed 41.8 per cent of Belgian male workers in 1910, and at around that date 26.5 per cent of French, 38.5 per cent of German, 12.8 per cent of Russian and 45.5 per cent of British. In terms of structural change in the male labour force, Britain was more 'industrialized' than Germany. Incidentally, by comparing the above data with Table 2 you will get an idea of the relative productivity of different sectors in different countries: in Russia, for example, the output of manufacturing was proportionately much greater than the size of the manufacturing labour force, a result of the capital intensity of Russian industry and the low productivity of agriculture. The relatively low productivity of agriculture is also evident from the British data where eleven and a half per cent of men worked on the land in 1911, but the proportion of agriculture in total output was much lower.

French women were more likely to be employed outside the home than in any other European country: in 1906, some 39 per cent of females were reckoned economically active, compared with about 25 per cent in Britain and Germany. The ratio of male to female workers in French manufacturing was 3:2, compared with only 3:1 in Germany and 2:1 in Britain. You will recall John Golby's discussion of the demographic stagnation of later nineteenth-century France in Unit 7, and will already have deduced that women's high participation ratio in paid employment resulted from the chronic labour shortage in industry and the retention of large numbers of men on the land.

One European economic community or many national economies?

Our aims for the unit (above), presuppose that Europe was a congeries (aggregation) of national economies and that its major political units provide the most analytically useful frameworks for the economic historian. This cannot pass without scrutiny. It is true that the essential data on employment, output and income come to us in national accounts, and this is one reason why modern economic history is written in 'national' terms, but the idea that the nation state is the most appropriate unit of analysis is challengeable.

No one has challenged it more effectively than Professor Pollard who has argued that industrialization was a process of technological transfer from *region to region*. Some regions spanned national borders (an example is the iron-working region in the Belgian and French Ardennes), and the wider context of regional development was not the nation state but a single European economic community. He conceives of the innovative British techniques diffusing like a disease from a common source after about 1820, and infecting first localities in 'Inner Europe' (Northern France, Belgium, the Rhineland) that were specifically hospitable to the germ. In its earliest phases, he suggests, governments were at best irrelevant, and frequently took a negative part, in an epidemic spread in 'civil society'.

The disease analogy is somewhat unfortunate: industrial societies are, literally, healthier than their predecessors. More seriously, the geographical and economic divisions between 'Inner' Europe (where the new technologies were implanted by 1870) and 'Outer' Europe are imprecise. They are difficult to draw on a map, and not easy to define conceptually. Nevertheless, the overall argument is compelling. All agree that industrialization was initially highly localized, because of the need to site factories near power sources (a map of early industrial Britain is a guide to its then known coal fields.) But for Pollard, an industrial region has a much greater economic significance, being an area with a distinct technological tradition, having its local capital resources, and enjoying a comparative advantage in the specialized production of commodities it traded with other parts of the country. 'National' accounts of economic growth disguise the fact that output soared in favoured industrial regions while it barely rose or stagnated in the national economy as a whole.

The key feature of the region, Pollard argues, is its *trading relationship to the rest of European society* (Pollard, 1981 p.113), an assertion which brings home the critical significance of commerce for industrialization. Europe's productive resources were undoubtedly more efficiently deployed, and economic growth accelerated as a result of inter-regional and international trade. It was easier to move goods between regions in industrializing Europe than labour and capital, and for this reason regions capitalized on natural endowments and other advantages to specialize in 'export' production of staple goods, and increase their technical efficiency by investing in coke-blast furnaces, steam engines and mechanized factories. 'Export' does not necessarily mean beyond international frontiers for in large states such as France specializing regions 'exported' mainly to the domestic national market. Hence the importance of road building in unifying the French national economy. But the two pioneer industrial regions in Britain and the Continent, Lancashire and the Sambre-Meuse valley, were distinctive in exporting a high proportion of their staple output beyond international frontiers. Their growth would not have been possible without the relatively efficient transport systems of Western Europe and ease with which goods could be internationally traded.

Britain and the 'Rostow' model

You should now watch again Video 2, Section 6, pp.748–920, and Section 8, pp.992–1158 before proceeding.

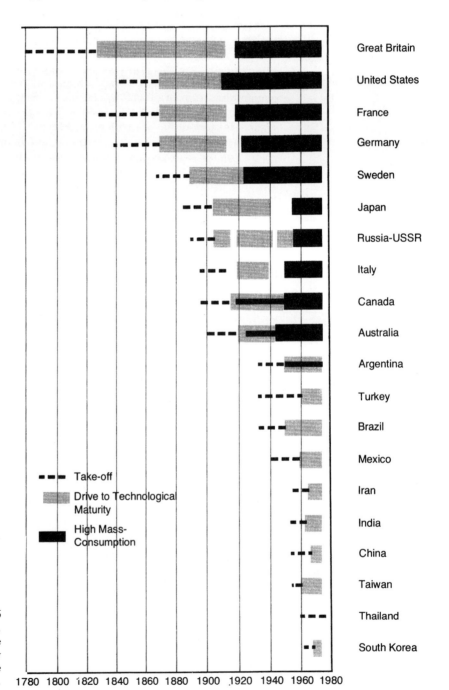

Figure 6
Stages of economic growth.
From W.W. Rostow, The
World Economy: History
and Prospect, *London, The
Macmillan Company, 1978.*

Since its publication in 1960, W. W. Rostow's *The Stages of Economic Growth* has had a considerable (though in recent years diminishing) influence on the conceptualization not only of Britain's Industrial Revolution, but of industrialization as such. Rostow proposed that the transition from 'traditional society' to self-sustained growth takes place through clearly defined stages and saw Britain as the 'paradigm case' whose experience was replicated, in broad terms, by later comers. During the 'preconditions stage' agriculture becomes more productive and surplus labour is freed for industrial employment; the market is extended by improvements in transport (canals and turnpike roads in Britain's case); and the financial services available to entrepreneurs become more sophisticated. The eye-catching metaphor in Rostow's scheme comes with the critical 'take-off' stage when the manufacturing sector lifts away from its economic base like an aircraft leaving the runway.

In a short period of time (two to three decades according to Rostow's original formulation), the rate of investment as a proportion of national income approximately doubles, certain major industries emerge as 'leading sectors' in the economy; and labour productivity rises on a scale which promotes radical technical changes in production, and hence further productivity increases and further investment in a self-perpetuating cycle. Once 'taken off', economies are launched on a 'drive to technological maturity' during which this cyclical process diffuses to all areas of the economy. The culminating stage in Rostow's scheme is that of 'High Mass Consumption' which, he argues, the United States entered just before the First World War and Britain and France just after. In the time chart (fig.6), Rostow's scheme is applied to a selection of countries.

You will note that, whereas Rostow first pinpointed Britain's 'take-off' very precisely to 1783–1802, his time chart indicates a much longer period for this critical phase (*c.*1780–*c.*1830). This revision in his thinking is consistent with the more recent quantitative work on Britain's Industrial Revolution which emphasizes the gradual nature of change and the accumulation of minor productivity gains over a long period of time. The economic historian who has done most to bring together and re-analyse the quantitative data is N.F.R. Crafts, in *British Economic Growth during the Industrial Revolution* (1985). Modern research findings used by Crafts indicate that, even by 1690, only a little over half the English labour force was in agriculture – a feature of the economy strikingly different from the general European experience (Crafts, 1985, p.17). By the mid-eighteenth century, manufacturing, building, commerce and the professions already accounted for about 45 per cent of labour force allocation. The structural shift from 'primary' to 'secondary' sectors was substantially complete by 1841:

Table 4: Distribution of the British Labour Force

	I	II	III	IV	V
1801	35.9	29.7	11.2	11.5	11.8
1841	22.2	40.5	14.2	14.5	8.5

Key
I = Agriculture, Forestry, Fishing,
II = Manufactures, Mining, and Industry,
III = Trade and Transport
IV = Domestic and Personal,
V = Public, Professional and all others

Source: Deane and Cole, 1962; cited in Crafts, 1985, p.15

Within this structural shift, there were major changes in the relative importance of different industries in total manufacturing output. In 1770, wool and leather accounted for over half the value added in British industry, and cotton for only 2.6 per cent. By 1831, the share of cotton in total value added had risen to 22.4 per cent, that of wool and leather had declined to 23 per cent. Over the same period, the prices of cotton goods had fallen substantially, while woollen and leather prices had risen. Does this confirm Rostow's concept of a 'leading sector'? Superficially, yes. No econometric revisionism can disguise the 'explosive acceleration' (Crafts, 1985, p.24) in cotton output. Furthermore, cotton mechanization long constituted the principal demand for steam power.

But, fundamentally, econometric analysis exposes the limitations of Rostow's metaphor: cotton was too small a sector to act as the engine of 'lift off'. Cotton enterprises had a low capital threshold – meaning limited demands on investment resources – and made few backward linkages to other sectors (such as iron). Since Rostow's *Stages*, it has been demonstrated that the doubling of the rate of investment took much longer than the two decades originally designated the 'take off' years. As a proportion of GNP, British domestic investment rose from 6 per cent of GNP to 11.7 per cent between 1760 to 1830 – (Crafts, 1985, Table 4.1, p.73) – further evidence of gradual, piecemeal change.

Economists have usually identified investment as a key source of economic growth and you might infer that the figures confirm its importance 'over the long term'. In fact, all attempts to 'partition' the sources of growth between new investment and greater productivity from all inputs into production indicate that the latter's contribution was three times greater. That is to say, some sixty per cent of the growth of the British economy between 1760 and 1830 is attributable to productivity increases (in other words, employing existing techniques more effectively and driving labour harder) and about twenty per cent to the rising rate of investment (which meant spending more on capital goods for each worker). Indeed, just to maintain the existing ratio between capital stock and labour, every annual increase of one per cent in population would have had to be matched by an extra 2.5 per cent of national income devoted to investment to compensate. The indications are that the growth of investment was scarcely sufficient to keep pace with demographic expansion *and* maintain capital–labour ratios.

In 'partitioning' the sources of growth, the final twenty per cent has been attributed to *technical change* – most notably the famous cluster of innovations in textiles and iron and steel manufacture. What might surprise you is how small the contribution of innovation to aggregate economic growth was. But if we divide the labour force between industries where technique had been 'revolutionized' by 1841, and those where it was unchanged (building, food and drink, leather etc.), then less than one in five workers would be counted as employed in the 'revolutionized' sector. The famous inventions which brought tremendous productivity increases in iron and steel and textiles should not blind us to the fact that around 1850 much of the economy remained small scale, little affected by the use of steam power and where labour productivity was no greater than in Continental Europe.

So what's left of Rostow's model? In the British context not much. If Crafts's estimates are sound, Rostow and other writers were empirically mistaken about the overall growth rate of the economy which did not reach 3 per cent of GNP per year before 1830 (Crafts, 1985, p.47). This was much slower than the growth rates achieved by later industrializing countries. When we bear in mind that population was increasing rapidly, then the annual per capita increase in GNP in the first third of the nineteenth century works out at about half a per cent. The acceleration in the growth rate was so drawn out and productivity improvements for so long concentrated in relatively few industries as to make the 'take off' metaphor inapt.

Moreover, far from being a paradigm case, British industrial development was in many ways atypical of Europe. One distinctive feature was that a large proportion of increased output was exported: by 1840 manufactures accounted for 90 per cent of British exports when the country was already importing substantial quantities of foodstuffs; cotton textiles alone made up four-tenths of exports in the first half of the nineteenth century. When France and Germany were at a comparable level of industrial development in 1870, manufactures were only 53 per cent of their exports. More fundamentally, the transfer of productive resources from the primary to the secondary sector was completed very early, and in advance of generalized technical change. The 'real' revolution lay in the establishment of capitalist agriculture, the concentration of landed property in a small élite, and the expulsion of redundant labour from the countryside. With the culmination of the centuries-long enclosure movement between 1750 and 1835, access to land and income from land came to be denied to great numbers of the rural labour force. However, the productivity of those who remained in agriculture rose well above French (and other European) agricultural labour. There were numerous conduits through which agricultural rents and profits could be diverted into Britain's urban economy, and such flows encouraged the migration of surplus rural labour. Altogether, the conditions for that structural change which provides our second definition of industrialization were ideal.

Britain, it is now evident, followed one path of development which other countries, such as France, avoided. What the welfare gains and losses of this path were is a difficult question. British wage levels were the highest in Europe throughout the nineteenth century but the 'costs' of urban life in terms of the pollution, congestion and chronic housing shortage on which so many Continental observers commented were also high. These 'disamenities' of *laissez faire* urban living were not imposed on the majority of French people who remained far longer in the countryside where land ownership was widely dispersed and economic inequality was much less pronounced than in Britain. (An argument made forcefully in O'Brien and Keyder, 1978, pp.186–8.)

After 1850, services, not manufacturing, were the most dynamic sector in the British economy and Britain's economic global hegemony rested on the export of development capital to the rest of the world, a near monopoly of international shipping and communications, and the provision of financial and commercial services. Of course, Britain developed an array of highly successful industries from marine engineering and shipbuilding to bicycles, and long remained the world's leading exporter of manufactures. But we must remember that later nineteenth-century Britain was an *import-oriented* economy whose chronic imbalance in commodity trade was corrected only by the inflow of income earned on capital invested abroad. Between 1865 and 1899 Britain exported only £499 million pounds worth of goods to France, its nearest large market; French exports to Britain in the same period were worth £1,458 millions (calculated from Mitchell, 1992, p.644). French tariffs were not a significant factor in this commercial imbalance which was proportionately as great in the free-trading 1860s as in the protectionist 1890s. British exporters were simply not making the high value-added products which bourgeois consumers wanted to buy.

Is this a symptom of that 'decline' which is so often and so unthinkingly projected back into the British past? Only if we imagine that there was some pinnacle of industrial dynamism attained by early nineteenth-century entrepreneurs. The more realistic picture of industrializing Britain.

> [I]s of an economy in much of which productivity growth was very slow and in which much manufacturing remained traditional and rather little affected by productivity change ... Further, if the economy was not pervasively innovative [and enjoyed only a relatively brief period of rapid productivity growth in the mid-nineteenth century], then Britain's relative decline in the face of growing economic competition after 1870 may also be rather less puzzling than otherwise. (Crafts, 1985 p.87)

The entrepreneurial failure often perceived in late nineteenth-century Britain would seem to be no more than illusion created by ill-conceived notions of an earlier industrial dynamism.

Relative economic backwardness

You should now view again Video 2, Section 9, pp.1159–446.

Revisionist work on the British Industrial Revolution necessarily has a bearing on how we conceptualize the industrialization of the Continental economies. Since they industrialized some decades later by adopting British technology they were by definition relatively 'backward'. But if, as Crafts and others contend, the pace of British advance has been exaggerated, then the degree of 'backwardness' and the effort required to catch up were, in reality, correspondingly less. Textbook accounts often overestimate the economic gap between Britain and France in the early nineteenth century, for example, and tend to conflate variation from the path followed by the British economy with retardation.

Nevertheless, the concept of relative economic backwardness is essential to understanding the industrialization of the 'follower' economies. The term was coined by Alexander Gerschenkron (1904–78), one of the first to analyse the ways 'late' industrializers overcame their historic disadvantages. What he offered economic historians was a *typology* enabling them to relate certain well-defined characteristics of industrialization in different countries to the timing of the process and, more importantly, the different levels of economic development from which they began to create modern industry. The typology was suggested by comparison of the German states (where industrialization began c.1830/50) with two laggard states, Russia and Italy, where industrial growth 'took off' during the 1890s. The latter economies, in particular, lacked what Rostow and others regarded as prerequisites for industrialization (such as an efficient, market-oriented agriculture and sophisticated financial institutions), and public authorities had to create 'substitutes' for what in Britain had arisen autonomously. Gerschenkron argued that the more backward the economy at the onset of industrialization:

- the smaller the contribution made by agriculture as a market for industrial goods;
- the greater would be the initial acceleration or 'spurt' in the rate of growth of industrial output;
- the greater the stress on producers' goods industries (such as iron and steel), large-scale plant and industrial monopolies;
- greater pressure would be placed on the living standards of the masses whose consumption would 'squeezed' to help finance industrialization (thus the Russian peasantry were purportedly highly taxed to pay the interest on the foreign loans raised for railway development);
- greater resort would be made to centralized methods of raising finance for industrialization (in moderately backward countries such as Germany these were industrial banks and in Russia, the state itself);
- finally, the more backward the country, then the more important the *ideologies* of industrialization in determining economic policy and choices. The ideas of the Comte de Saint-Simon (d.1825), who envisaged a rational, production-oriented society ruled by all who worked, have sometimes been seen as the 'industrializing' ideology of mid-nineteenth-century France, for example (Gerschenkron, 1962).

Not all of Gerschenkron's theses have been confirmed by subsequent research. The most recent statistical series for industrial output in Russia, Italy and the Habsburg Empire do not show discontinuities so abrupt as to warrant the term 'great spurts' (Sylla and Toniolo, 1991, p.6). As with Rostow's 'take-off', this is another instance where an attractive metaphor misleads. The industrialization process was smoother, more deeply rooted in the past, and by implication the pre-industrial landscapes from which industrialization grew less 'barren' than Gerschenkron believed. Nevertheless, his concept of 'relative backwardness' remains illuminating because it enables us to compare key features of the 'follower' economies within the same explanatory framework.

France: 'industrialization without an Industrial Revolution'?

In your video compilation, Michelle Perrot echoes a judgement first made by Sir John Clapham: 'In the course of the nineteenth century most French industries were remodelled, but it might be said that France never went through an industrial revolution' (Clapham, 1936, 1968 edn, p.53). The more recently compiled statistical series, showing the growth of industrial output since the eighteenth century, underline that conclusion for they exhibit no discontinuities of the kind posited by Rostow. Where the historical

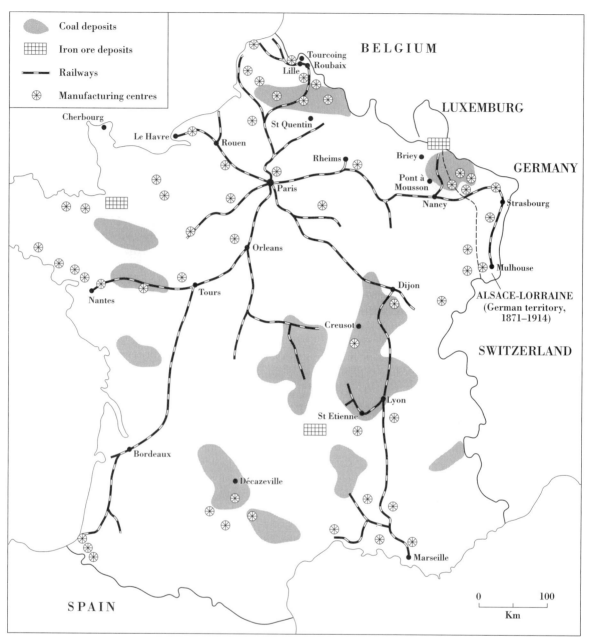

Figure 7
French industrial regions c.1870 showing major railway lines and main coalfields. (From C. Trebilcock, The Industrialization of the Continental Powers, 1780–1914, *Longman, London, 1981.)*

statisticians depart from Clapham's view is insisting on the very *early* start made by France as a manufacturing country; indeed, many now argue that the growth of this sector outpaced British development until *c.*1790 when revolution and war proved disastrous for proto-industrial regions heavily involved in overseas markets. To quote one authority:

[T]here was no true take-off in France at all: the growth of the French economy was very gradual and its origins lie far in the past ... the share of industry in physical product began to increase steadily from 1715–20 onwards ... for a number of historical reasons, the most important of which no doubt resides in the two countries' different agricultural structure, industrialization proceeded much more slowly in France and within narrower limits than was the case in England. (Marczewski, 1963, p.129, also cited in Fohlen, 1973, p.12)

Some measure of the stately pace of French industrialization can be gained from the calculation that, in 1870, some 85 per cent of the gross manufacturing output came from the more traditional industries which had not moved towards modern concentrated production and where technical progress had been limited.

Before analysing why the industrialization process in France was slower and more restricted than in Britain, three points must be emphasized:

1   In 1800, France was the second most populous European country, and during the 1830s her population still exceeded that of the German states by about 10 per cent. For this reason alone, the absolute size of her manufacturing sector was bound to be comparatively large, but we must bear in mind too that agrarian wealth and prosperous commercial towns meant a large domestic market. Until the early 1860s, France was the world's second largest industrial power; it was only then that first the United States and then Germany overhauled her in terms of total manufacturing output. During the 1850s, the French rate of industrial growth had been amongst the highest in Europe.

2   The performance of the French economy over the nineteenth century, which has often been derogated as 'mediocre' by comparison with Britain and Germany, appears in a different light if we compare *per capita* growth in output and productivity, rather than aggregate increases in national products. The reason for this lies in France's distinctive demographic experience: her population grew by less than a third between 1801 and 1851, and a mere 9 per cent between 1851 and 1914, and growth of GNP was consequently slower than in economies where the labour force expanded rapidly. It has been calculated that the annual growth rate in physical output (at constant prices) in France from the 1810s to the 1900s was 1.5 per cent, while in Britain it was 2.6 per cent. But the British population trebled in this period, so per capita growth in output was 1.3 per cent; in France it was 1.2 per cent. Average real incomes increased by roughly the same amount in both societies (Crouzet, 1974, p.169, citing the statistical work of J. Marczewski, W. A. Cole and P. Deane).

3   Despite problems of labour supply, France enjoyed a period of rapid growth in 1896–1913 when the annual increase in industrial output was 2.4 per cent and French entrepreneurs established a commanding place in a key industry of the Second Industrial Revolution: motor-vehicles. The French industry was the largest in Europe in 1914 and the world's leading exporter. The biggest firm, Renault, was already introducing Henry Ford's assembly-line techniques, as well as the managerial practices associated with F. W. Taylor. Other sectors were equally innovative in employing advanced technology: France became Europe's leading aluminium producer thanks to a combination of abundant ore, invention (Paul Heroult's electrolytic process, patented 1886), and the

exploitation of hydro-electric power in the Alps. The same metallurgist devised an electric furnace for the manufacture of special steels. As the birth-rate was falling to a nadir during this period of industrial expansion, we must be cautious about invoking the demographic factor in explaining the slow growth of the 1860s and 1870s, and the stagnation of the 1880s.

Exercise   I quoted above the widely-shared judgement that France's agricultural structure led to industrialization being a slower process than in Britain; why was this? There is also general agreement that a natural resource deficiency impeded the adoption of many of the technical processes associated with 'the First Industrial Revolution'; what was this deficiency?

Discussion   As I am sure you have grasped, the key factor was the size and stability of the peasant population whose rights of ownership and freedom from feudal exactions had been secured by the French Revolution. Because French law prescribed equal inheritance amongst all male heirs, peasants preserved their patrimony by family limitation. The consequences for the *supply* side of the economy have already been mentioned in terms of labour, and there were significant ramifications for capital, too. Savings tended to be attracted to landed property rather than industrial investment. Moreover, small and medium urban entrepreneurs only a generation or two away from the land were steeped in a culture of 'Malthusianisme' (a word adopted into French to describe voluntary limitation of output in the economy, as well as the bed-chamber): they avoided risk-taking and innovation, were keener to preserve control over family businesses than 'go for growth' by public flotation.

Some historians have given more emphasis to the different *demand* constraints imposed by a large and stable peasantry, arguing that low rates of internal migration meant a less hospitable internal market for factory-made goods than the wage-earning masses in British cities. The French bourgeoisie probably consumed a larger share of French industry than their British counterparts did of their own industry and were likely to be more sensitive to quality and style than wage earners and *manoeuvriers* (O'Brien and Keyder, 1978). There is a further point to consider: while the security of their property was a blessing for most peasants most of the time, during the long agricultural depression of the late nineteenth century, farms could be millstones round the necks of the more enterprising who wanted to sell up and leave the land. With the fall in prices, and the devastation of vineyards by phylloxera from the mid-1870s, the market in agricultural land was very depressed, and peasants could not obtain a price that compensated them for capital and labour they had invested.

The resource which fuelled industrialization *à la britannique* was coal, in which France is poorly endowed. As Figure 8 (p.97) shows, per capita consumption of coal in France was the lowest of the four western European industrial powers throughout the nineteenth century, and about a third of the total consumed had to be imported. This alone made coke-fuelled iron-smelting processes more expensive in France, and prolonged archaic techniques: charcoal-fired forges attained their peak output in 1837, and still produced about half of all pig iron in 1850. Where French coal was available, it was often located some distance from iron ore reserves. The fuel costs of steam power were comparatively so high as to give an incentive to innovation in the use of water power: the result was the highly efficient hydraulic turbine (see the time chart, above, p.80). As late as 1899, some 56 per cent of the horsepower of *newly installed* prime movers came from hydraulic motors (Cameron, 1985, p.14; my emphasis). Cameron notes:

> [T]he characteristics of water as a source of power imposed constraints upon its use. The best locations were generally remote from centres of population; the number of users at any given location was limited to one or a very few; the size of the installations was similarly limited. Thus, important though water power was for French industrialization, the resulting pattern included small firm size, geographical dispersion of industry and slow urbanization, characteristics displayed also by other coal-poor industrial nations. (Cameron, 1985, p.14)

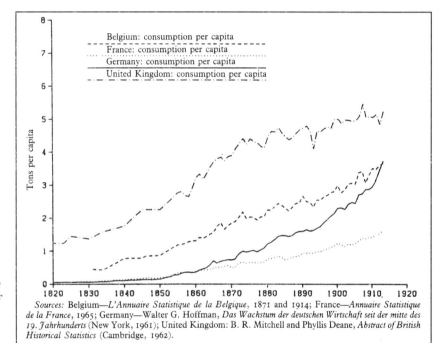

Figure 8
Per capita consumption of coal in France, Britain, Belgium and Germany. (From Cameron, 1985).

Sources: Belgium—*L'Annuaire Statistique de la Belgique*, 1871 and 1914; France—*Annuaire Statistique de la France*, 1965; Germany—Walter G. Hoffman, *Das Wachstum der deutschen Wirtschaft seit der mitte des 19. Jahrhunderts* (New York, 1961); United Kingdom: B. R. Mitchell and Phyllis Deane, *Abstract of British Historical Statistics* (Cambridge, 1962).

Transport

One might also speculate that the coal deficiency, and comparative unfamiliarity with steam technology, contributed to France's relative tardy railway development: in 1860, in relation to total population and territorial size, the country was under-supplied with railways compared with the German states, Belgium and Switzerland (Pollard, 1981, Table 3.2, p.108). There were certainly other, probably more important factors: dispute as to whether construction was to be undertaken by the state at public expense or, as in Britain, by private enterprise, delayed the passage of the key railway law until 1842. A 'mixed economy' was instituted under which the central state, interested *départements* and *communes*, and concessionary speculative companies co-operated. Two-thirds of the cost of the land required was borne by local government; the other third by the central state which also undertook the embanking and earth-works. The companies bore the cost of the rails, rolling stock and the operating expenses of the lines. This was probably the best compromise available given that large-scale capital formation was more difficult in France than Britain, but the resulting network fell short of optimal economic efficiency. Towns and regions which would have benefited from market integration remained unconnected because they could not raise their share of the costs; others were connected for 'political' reasons. Many of the first concessionary companies were under-capitalized and unable to pay their way. The economic and revolutionary crises of 1847–8 slowed down the rate of construction, which did not revive until 1851 when the railways were moving only about 11 per cent of the total volume transported. Alsace, the premier cotton manufacturing region did not receive its first delivery of raw cotton by rail until 1852. Not until 1857 did the tonnage transported by rail exceed that moved by water. Hitherto, the road-building programme of the July monarchy (which brought, on average, 1,326 kilometres of national highway into use per year between 1831 and 1847) had been far more significant in integrating the national space into a common market than the railways. The peak railway investment decade was 1855–64 when construction demands for iron and machinery exerted a major galvanizing effect on the economy and the balance in the transport 'mix' shifted decisively to the railways. By 1876, they were carrying 63 per cent of the tonnage transported. Even then, large regions of France remained relatively isolated and poorly integrated into the national economic 'space'. Despite the effort made to integrate the isolated regions with the rest of the country under the Freycinet public works plan launched in 1878, transport provision in rural France was still sparser than elsewhere in western Europe in the early twentieth century: there was, in 1907, just under 1 km of railway in Belgium for every 3 square miles of territory, in Britain the ratio was around 1:4, in Germany 1:6, and in France 1:8.

Imitations of, and 'deviations' from the British model

France poses problems for those, such as Professor Pollard, who argue that 'the industrialization of Europe took place on the British model; it was, as far as the Continent was concerned, purely and deliberately an imitative process' (Pollard, 1981, p.v). One problem is that the use of yardsticks derived from the British economy, in which supply and demand conditions were so different, leads to under-rating the French industrial performance. Another, that the model encourages us to dismiss as 'deviant' (or neglect altogether) distinctive features of French industrialization that cannot plausibly be attributed to relative backwardness.

One instance is the different direction in which the process of *industrial integration* proceeded in France, as compared with Britain. Where allied branches of the same sector (such as spinning and weaving in textiles) are brought together in the same firm (though not necessarily under the same roof) then we have business integration. Industrial production is conventionally pictured as a 'stream' whose 'source' is raw materials and whose 'outlet' the goods sold to consumers. From this, we designate industries 'upstream' or 'downstream'. Business integration occurred in both Britain and France during industrialization but, as M. Lévy-Leboyer showed, not in the same way. In Britain, integration originated with heavy, 'upstream' industries which turned out intermediate and producer goods, and later extended into 'downstream' processes. In France, integration began amongst firms producing finished articles and worked 'upstream'. The explanation would appear to be that, for French consumer goods manufacturers, inputs of raw-materials and semi-manufactures were a much greater proportion of their total costs than was the case in Britain, where wages were higher. To control their costs, they began to integrate with 'up-stream' producers. To give an example, in the Alsace cotton industry integration was initiated by dyers and printers of cotton who bought into weaving and then spinning to reduce costs and maintain competitiveness. All the major firms in the region emerged in this way, which was quite different from Lancashire's (Lévy-Leboyer, 1968).

Pollard gives pride of place to technological diffusion in his account of European industrialization, and there were numerous recorded instances of French industrialists imitating British innovations in textiles and iron and steel manufacture. (Indeed, the expressions 'mule-jenny', 'coke' and 'coking' were adopted into French for this reason.) But since these sectors never acquired the same weight in the French economy, the imitation can seem 'pale' or half-hearted. However, Pollard's diffusionist model neglects the innovations – of French origin – in areas of manufacturing that were relatively much more important to France than to Britain. The high-quality printing of cloth, at which the French excelled, was transformed by rolling machines that allowed for the use of up to six colours. France was similarly in the technological vanguard of high-quality paper-making. Though 'haute couture' may not seem to us the stuff of an industrial revolution, it was a very profitable business in which the 'comparative advantage' of the leading French houses was unassailable (among other things, the finest silks, cottons and linens were home-produced). Bonnet-making was revolutionized by new looms of French design. 'Imitation' was unquestionably one element in French industrialization, but indigenous creativity was just as important.

By 1850, the effects of imitation were most evident in mining, metallurgy and mechanized cotton spinning, and were not simply matters of technology. French visitors to the big industrial establishments in Lancashire and the Midlands were struck by their superior organization, the stricter division of labour between different shops and departments, and the centralization of decision-taking. To quote one French historian 'They took away with them the idea of the 'rationalized' firm' (Léon, 1976, p.504). Coal mining grew in scale because the deeper seams being exploited required concentrations of fixed capital and labour; by 1851, fifteen companies employed half the total work force, and two large concerns – the Compagnie (Cie) Anzin and the Cie des Mines de la Loire – accounted for nearly half of total national coal output. This monopoly power was so alarming to the government that measures were instituted to slow down the concentration process. In iron and steel, large-size firms were created through the fusion of small enterprises, and some integrated with mining and engineering concerns; by 1870, the ten largest firms were producing 55 per cent of total output. Numerous artisanal firms stayed in business, but each with an output of less than one per cent of the largest company, Le Creusot.

Concentration of employment in cotton spinning was greatest in Alsace where eighteen of the spinning mills employed 200 to 1000 workers in 1840–4, and the average number per enterprise was 290. By contrast, the average number of workers in the spinning mills of the Nord and Seine-

Inférieure was 100 and 80 respectively. The difference is explained by the fact that Alsatian industry was more highly capitalized and technologically advanced, and retained this position up to the 1870s (when the province was annexed by Germany). The industry developed originally on the basis of water-power from the Vosges, but made a rapid transition to steam, with the consequence that the number of spindles per establishment rose from 9,517 in 1827 to 17,969 in 1856 and then to 24,400 in 1869. Cotton weaving remained a predominantly rural handicraft in 1850, with a relatively small proportion of production accounted for by mechanized factories that averaged around 100–200 workers. In the other textile trades, concentration proceeded much more slowly: in 1881, the national average number of power looms per establishment was 125 in the cotton industry, 39 in the woollen, and 41 in hemp and flax.

The causes of decelerated growth and stagnation after 1860

One further problem the French economy poses for a diffusionist model was the perceptible deceleration of industrial growth around 1860, just at the point when the railways were exercising a palpable influence on the economy. In Britain the mid-Victorian boom continued until the early 1870s, and in Germany and Belgium industrial expansion accelerated. Why was France anomalous? Several factors were probably important, but two appear to have acted in an unfortunate conjunction. Labour and skill shortages became quite chronic in some industries, as we can deduce from the expedients (company housing, the allotment of employees' gardens, the founding of technical schools) adopted to get workers to renounce their 'nomadism' and upgrade their skills. Secondly, the liberal trade policy followed after the 1860 Cobden treaty disadvantaged French manufacturing where it competed with Britain, but greatly benefited wine-growers and other agriculturists. The course of French industrialization after 1815 underlines that protection was a necessary condition for growth in the basic industries in which the economy was otherwise disadvantaged by fuel shortages. The free trade interlude of the 1860s, in a generally protectionist commercial policy throughout the nineteenth century, gave peasants an added incentive to stay on the land. So profitable did wine become, that certain regions, such as the department of Hérault, made a wholesale switch from manufacturing to wine-growing: 'This was no small-scale agricultural change but the veritable *de-industrialization* of a whole region of the country; an area with a long established industrial base became a 'sea of vines' (Milward and Saul, 1977, p.110; my emphasis).

The retarding influences were amplified by the territorial losses of 1871: with Alsace-Lorraine went rich textile industries, important caches of minerals, and no less than four-fifths of the entire French machine-building industry. Iron ore deposits making up 80 per cent of known French resources were surrendered, together with their attendant blast-furnaces and steelworks. After the world-wide financial crash of 1873, all industrial economies grew more slowly (compared with the mid-century boom), but in France the stagnant sectors and regions exercised a notably depressing effect, masking the dynamism of industrial centres like Le Creusot. With agriculture still the largest source of income for the French people, the *pébrine* and phylloxera that devastated silk and wine-growing from the later 1870s were national economic disasters. Farming families' incomes were reduced and demand for consumer goods fell. A heroic investment effort had to go into re-stocking French vineyards. The level of industrial investment dropped below that required to compete internationally, a shortfall compounded by the preferences of French investors for guaranteed state bonds and foreign securities.

The persistence of small-scale, family enterprise

The tenacity of small-scale enterprise in industrializing Europe is a commonplace of economic history, but for particular reasons France exhibited this characteristic more strongly than the other major economies. Even in the later 1920s, large-scale units of production (i.e. those comprising more than 500 employees) accounted for only 19 per cent of wage earners in industry; by comparison, 50 per cent of Germany's industrial and mining labour force was already concentrated in installations of more than 500 workers in 1914 (Fohlen, 1978; Trebilcock, 1981, p.69).

As we have noted, big mines and factories were created, but employment in *new* small enterprises rose at nearly the same rate so that the shift in the distribution of the labour force away from workshop and craft production was very protracted. The 1851 census classified manufacturing into *grande industrie* and *petite industrie*; in the first, 124,000 employers and 1,300,000 dependent workers were enumerated (an average of eleven workers per business); in the second, the census recorded 1,550,000 *maîtres* with 2,800,000 workers (roughly two workers for every employer on average). A survey of 1872 indicates that no change in the overall business structure had occurred despite the industrial expansion during the Second Empire. What were classified as 'factories and manufactures' were employing on average less than ten workers per business and in 'small industries' there were fewer than two workers for every employer.

The industrial census of 1896 showed that for each 100 industrial establishments, 83 employed one to four workers, 13 employed from five to fifty, and 4 employed more than 50 wage earners. Though the figures confirm that the small firm was the backbone of the French economy, employment was, nevertheless, tending to concentrate in bigger firms: 40 per cent of industrial workers were employed by that four per cent of firms which could be described as 'medium sized or larger'.

However, what greatly complicates the received notion of business structure in early twentieth-century France is data indicating that in two key sectors, coal mining and metallurgy, *the average size of enterprises was the largest in western Europe*. In French coal mining in 1906, there were on average 984 workers per company (compared with 163.5 in Germany), while in French metallurgy there were 711 workers (compared with 141.6 in Germany) (Stearns, 1975, p.155). To reconcile the mining figures with the 1872 survey, we must presume a rapid rate of company merger in the French coal fields at the end of the century. Assuming that the data are genuinely comparable, and that business size correlated positively with the size of units of production, then we have the intriguing question as to why French collieries and steelworks were so much bigger on average than German. The explanation might be that the geological difficulties of mining coal in France, and the problems of maintaining an economic supply of coke in steel-making, meant that the only enterprises which could succeed in these sectors were those which achieved great economies of scale.

The predominance of small- and medium-scale enterprises was long regarded as the prime cause of France's purportedly lacklustre industrial performance, and explanations for it often smacked of the prosecutor's charge sheet. The excessive prudence of entrepreneurs, their refusal to resort to institutional credit, and fear of risk-taking – all supposedly derived from the pervasive climate of 'Malthusianisme' – were arraigned. The fact that industrialists preferred to raise capital from within the family and a narrow circle of close associates, and that most industrial expansion was financed out of profits, were added to the charges. Extenuating circumstances entered on behalf of the industrialist have been the withdrawal of the major financial institutions (such as Crédit Lyonnais) from industrial investment, and excessive foreign investment in under-developed economies that were poor markets for French goods. Now that the performance of the French economy is recognized as 'creditable', the prosecution's case has collapsed; it would seem rather more reasonable to credit small firms for some of the 'flexibility and vigour' on display throughout the nineteenth century. (The quoted expressions are in Crouzet, 1974, p.179.) In truth, there were two categories of enterprise in nineteenth-century France: alongside antiquate workshops that had long re-paid (or 'amortized') their investment in plant and machinery were enterprises at the cutting edge of technical progress. Family firms figured in both; dynastic control did not exclude expansion and innovation. The social matrix of the Alsatian cotton industry was a network of Protestant families proud of their independence of banking and public capital. Better-known dynasties are the Schneiders (armament manufacturers), the de Wendels (steel founders) and the Michelins (rubber tyres and gastronomic guides). These dynasties carried secretive habits (born of their family character) into the twentieth century: de Wendel, for example, did not appeal to the financial market until 1908, and preferred raising money in Germany (where company law was laxer) in order not to disclose balance-sheets and statutes.

Though large-scale industrial enterprises were nowhere common before the later nineteenth century, it is true that the legal framework was more of an obstacle to big business in France until 1867 (when limited liability was enacted). French legislators were suspicious of joint-stock organization – which was considered dangerously speculative and liable to defraud the public – and imposed strict conditions on public company registration. The legal forms of corporate enterprise were the 'simple partnership', the 'limited partnership', and the joint-stock company. The first – normally a registered agreement amongst relatives – was easily the most popular: over three-quarters of the 67,500 companies formed between 1848 and 1867 were simple partnerships, just over a fifth limited partnerships, and only 307 were joint-stock companies. Of these, only a tiny number were manufacturing enterprises. Comparison with Germany (and Belgium) where joint-stock manufacturing companies were important during and after the 'take-off' decades, would indicate that a reluctance to call on private investors was implicated in the 'minutiarization' of French industry. Again by comparison with Belgium and Germany, the French capital market was slow to develop before mid-century, and though investment banks were founded from the 1830s, their role did not match that of the Belgian *Société Générale* or the German financial institutions. Hoarding and investment in landed property were common amongst the wealthy and at least until the 1860s industrial investment seemed less secure and less prestigious than the mortgage market. The most heavily capitalized French companies in 1881 were in railway transport, shipping, mining and public utilities; the largest manufacturer, Le Creusot steel, ranked only eighteenth in the land.

Germany's path to industrial supremacy

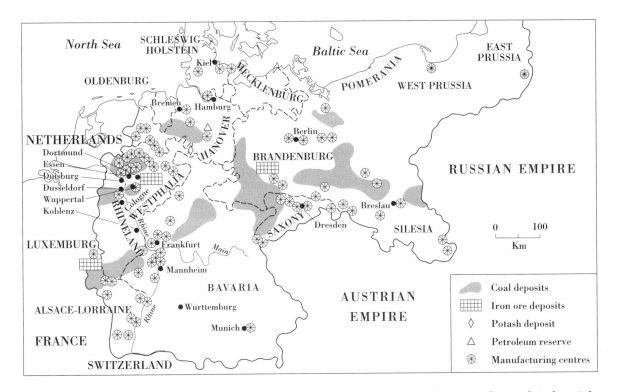

Figure 9
German industrial regions,
c.1900. (The map also
shows the political
divisions between the states
of the German Empire
after 1871.) (From
Trebilcock, 1981.)

By 1913, Germany was Europe's largest, and most advanced industrial economy by far. Her steel output exceeded that of her European rivals combined, as did the amount of electric energy she produced. Her greatest industrial achievement was an organic chemicals industry whose dyestuffs products totalled four-fifths of world output. Many of the 'plastic' derivatives of cellulose were first synthesized in the industrial research laboratories of the giant German firms before 1914. In another high technology industry, electrical engineering, German pre-eminence was almost as striking: German goods accounted for half the international trade in electrical products in 1913 (Landes, 1969, pp.275–276; Trebilcock, 1981, p.47). This rise to the leadership of the Second Industrial Revolution had been astonishingly rapid. Rostow's chart, you will note, dates the German 'take-off' to between the late 1830s and 1870, while others have argued for the 1850s as the decade when the critical acceleration of the growth of modern scale-intensive industrial production began (Trebilcock, 1981, p.38). Even so, on the eve of the Franco-Prussian war, Prussia was still an overwhelmingly agrarian society, with only 26 per cent of its population living in communities of 2,000 or more. Between 1880 and 1913, the output of the German industrial economy approximately quadrupled, while in both Britain and France it only doubled. The German rate of industrial growth after 1900 was matched only by Italy, but by then Germany was a mature industrial economy and Italy a relatively 'underdeveloped' society still in the first phase of industrialization. To achieve these increases in output, German society was re-cast: the labour reserves of the industrializing regions were quite insufficient and from the 1880s a massive movement of population brought German and Slav workers from East Prussia and Tsarist Russia to the Ruhr, industrial Saxony and Silesia. Regional discrepancies in living standards accentuated; though 'dualism' was not as acute as in Italy, parts of impoverished East Elbia came to resemble the Italian South.

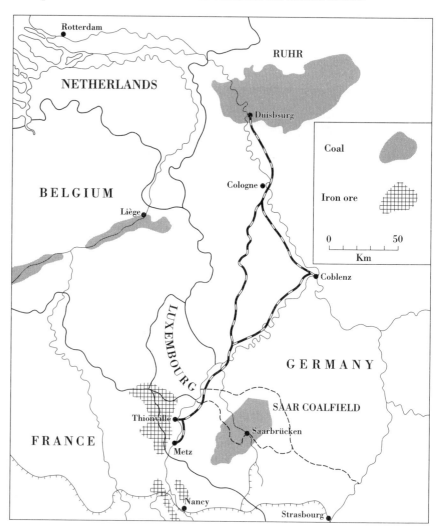

Figure 10
Major coal and iron deposits in the west of the German Empire, c. 1900. (From N.J.G. Pounds, An Historical Geography of Europe 1800–1914, 1985, Cambridge University Press, Cambridge, 1985.)

Now, one view might be that to ask what explains the rise of the German states from comparative backwardness to industrial pre-eminence is to pose the wrong question. The real problem is explaining why industrialization began so late, or identifying the impediments to 'take off' before 1850. To play devil's advocate for a moment, the combination of natural resource endowments, labour and capital inputs, political regimes securing property rights and an international context facilitating technological transfer, were sufficient to ensure industrialization. And since this combination was, fortuitously, close to optimal in the German states, there is no need to look for a 'special route' to German industrial success. Special pleading, no doubt, but it is true there were copious supplies of coal in the Ruhr, limited deposits of iron ore (supplemented after 1871 by the acquisition of Lorraine), of potassium (an input to the chemicals industry), and navigable rivers which carried sea-borne goods into and out of the heart of Europe. The profits of agriculture and trade could be tapped for investment capital, and once the right financial institutions were in place the German states had little call for foreign investment. Patent registration meant other people's technological innovations could be quickly (and fairly) cheaply imported, a well-known instance being the adoption, after 1879, of the Thomas-Gilchrist process allowing for the utilization of phosphoric iron ores. The invention of basic steel was 'an event of world import' (Landes, 1969, p.259), but only because patent rights were leased to a handful of giant European firms almost as soon as the process was discovered. But the real clincher in the diabolic brief is the threefold demographic growth between 1800 and 1913 in the territory of the 1871 Reich. This created Europe's second most populous state, ensuring abundant supplies of labour and a constantly expanding market. Furthermore, the dissolution of feudal obligations (enacted in 1811) on terms highly advantageous to the land-owning aristocracy meant that surplus labour was easily 'pushed'

Table 5: Indices of Industrial Production (1871=100)

	Germany	Britain	France	Russia	Italy
1871	100	100	100	100	100
1880	124	116	120	183	108
1890	190	146	139	267	131
1900	290	184	164	525	156
1913	476	230	242	833	256

(Recalculated on an 1871 base, and rounded to the nearest whole number. It might appear that Russia grew faster than Germany and Italy after 1900, but if we make 1913=100, then the German and Italian indices for 1900 are both 61 and the Russian 63, indicating a slower rate of growth.)

Based on Mitchell, 1992, pp.409–11.

Table 6: Output of crude steel (000s metric tons)

	Germany	Britain	France	Russia	Italy
1871	143	334	84	7	-
1880	690	1,316	389	307	3
1890	2,135	3,636	683	378	108
1900	6,461	4,980	1,565	2,216	116
1913	17,609	7,787	4,687	4,918	934

Based on Mitchell, 1992, pp.456–7.

Table 7: Output of electric energy (in giga Watt hours)

	Germany	Britain	France	Russia	Italy
1900	1.0	0.2	0.34	-	0.14
1913	8.0	2.5	1.8	2.04	2.0

Based on Mitchell, 1992, p.546.

from agriculture into industry. Since the Prussian state was a pioneer of universal elementary education, there was the further advantage that human capital accumulated prior to 'take off', endowing new industries with literate work forces from which technical cadres could be drawn.

This devil's advocacy has much to commend it, but there are specious points amongst an otherwise valid argument. Whether German resource endowments were particularly rich is debatable, and we might argue that what was exceptional was the ability of German entrepreneurs to make the best of modest natural resources, some of which (e.g. potassium) only became important long after industrialization was in train. The adoption of the Thomas-Gilchrist process – some thirty years *after* 'take-off' you will have noted – could, in fact, be cited as an example of entrepreneurial expertise in overcoming natural deficiencies since it enabled the German steel industry to exploit an otherwise uneconomic resource (iron ore with a high phosphorous content). The devil's advocate seems to have slyly con-flated two distinct arguments in linking labour inputs to human capital. To be sure, abundant labour was a great advantage to German industry and important in keeping wages below those of her major international compet-itor, Britain, after the 1880s. This advantage came, as it were, 'naturally'. But human capital accumulated because Prussia's exceptional *educational policies* went far beyond the provision of elementary schooling. State-sup-port of technical instruction was remarkably far-sighted: between its founding in 1821 and 1850, the Berliner Gewerbe-Institut turned out 1,000 technically qualified students. Alumni included August Borsig (d.1854), a carpenter by trade who retrained as mechanic at the Institut and in 1837 established the engineering works where the first locos were built on Ger-man soil (Kocka, 1978, p.524; Sheehan, 1989, p.510). Other German states were less enlightened; sixty per cent of Bavarian adults were illiterate in the 1840s (Cameron, 1985, p.13).

Nevertheless, it is important not to 'mystify' the German industrial achievement and to recognize that the German states enjoyed certain his-toric advantages at the inception of industrialization. There were well-established and very enterprising mercantile groups in the Rhineland who had the requisite technical skills and business acumen to provide the first generation of industrialists in textiles and chemicals. Engineering entrepre-neurs could be recruited from the skilled metal-working craftsmen whose *Wanderjahre* ('wandering years') brought them into contact with new tech-niques and machines in western Europe. There were, too, advantages in the *timing* of the industrialization process as it occurred in Germany. The textiles phase of early industrialization was much more compressed (and the sector carried a smaller weight in the economy) than elsewhere. Entre-preneurs moved rapidly into the coal, iron and mechanical engineering industries at a time of hectic railway development, and the linkages between this leading sector (as it is deservedly called) and the new indus-tries were very strong. This timing meant that the German economy could reap the benefits of British industrial imports, but quickly substitute for them when its own capacity was up to scratch. By 1850 German iron-masters and loco builders were the main suppliers to the domestic market. Furthermore, the coincidence of early industrial growth with the national movement was propitious. Amongst liberal nationalists, industrialism was seen as fortifying the nation in its struggle for unity, and such many-sided entrepreneurs as Ludolf Camphausen (1803–90) and Gustav von Mevissen (1815–99), combined political careers with banking, transport, railway company promotion and industry. They represented 'an increasingly self-confident, organized and forward-looking bourgeoisie' who saw their entrepreneurial activity 'not only as means to personal success, but also as part of a national and civilizing mission' (Kocka, 1978, p.529). Some might even see an advantage in the Prussian state bureaucracy's 'enlightened' tradition of economic guidance: in late eighteenth-century Silesia, the state had acted as an entrepreneur by creating an iron industry, mainly to satisfy military needs. British technicians had been imported to advise on coke-blasting and iron-puddling. Elsewhere, however, the tradition of mercantilist enterprise and the free market economy of the Industrial Revolution did not mix: few of the state-favoured manufactories survived the economic liberalization which lifted the corporate restrictions on economic activity in the towns.

Exercise   So, what were the main impediments to industrialization in this expanding market of German people before the 1830s?

Discussion   You might have mentioned those vestiges of the old corporate order the craft guilds, whose privileges restricted economic innovation until freedom of enterprise was instituted (see Anderson, p.23). But business liberalization – *Gewerbefreiheit* – had begun during the Napoleonic occupation of the Rhineland and corporatism was a minor irritant in Prussia after 1830. The major impediment was the political fragmentation of Germany into 39 sovereign states, each with its own tariff regime, which meant that the market was poorly integrated. Goods transported from Hamburg to Austria had to traverse ten states and were subject to ten successive transit dues. The emergence of a regional division of labour – which Pollard sees as crucial to the industrialization process – was impeded wherever tariffs artificially raised the price of a region's manufactured exports.

This raises the question of the contribution to industrial growth of the German customs union *(Zollverein)*, created in 1834 by the larger states (though others acceded at later dates and members' commercial policies were not fully co-ordinated even in the 1860s). Internal tariff barriers were dismantled and the relatively low Prussian tariff of 1818 adopted as the common tariff in third-party trade. The Union owed much to the advocacy of Friedrich List (d.1846) whose *The National System of Political Economy* (1841) was an influential critique of the 'cosmopolitan' assumptions of British political economy. List particularly wished to refute David Ricardo's theory that nations should specialize in those economic activities in which they enjoyed an advantage in *'comparative costs'*. By the 1820s, the ratio of manufacturing to agricultural costs was so much lower in Britain than in Prussia that all parties to bilateral free trade would have gained from British specialization in textiles and Prussian in wheat. Indeed, something resembling this international division of labour was perceptible in the flow of Lancashire yarns and textiles into the German states and East Elbian wheat exports to Britain, though the Corn Laws and Prussian tariffs hindered the full flowering of reciprocal trade. List argued that since trading nations were at different stages of development, the practice of 'comparative advantage' (and free trade, its necessary corollary) would merely perpetuate Britain's lead in manufactures. List was a tireless opponent of trade barriers within central Europe, but wanted to retain a common German tariff to protect infant industries against British competition.

This rationale for the *Zollverein* has abetted a rather exaggerated estimation of its contribution to German industrial growth. Far from stifling infant industries, imports from Britain of intermediate goods – such as cotton yarn and pig iron – had provided cheap inputs for the earliest scale-intensive enterprises in Germany. To the degree that the *Zollverein's* common tariff restricted these imports, it hindered industrialization. True, the internal common market created by the Union was a precondition for national economic development, and there were economies of scale in the larger market for the first generation of textile industrialists. But the growth of a modern cotton industry tended to be at the expense of proto-industrial textile regions, so the net contribution of the customs union *per se* to aggregate demand and total manufacturing employment is very debatable. In fact, recent analyses argue that the 'gains' generated by the *Zollverein* were fiscal and political, rather than economic. Before 1834, tariffs had been the principal source of government income for many states, but the costs of collection had been high. With the Union, customs levied on international imports were pooled amongst member states who thereby achieved considerable economies of scale in revenue administration. As the volume of trade grew, and the proportion of gross revenue going on administration declined, so the conservative regimes were relieved of their fiscal dependence on constitutional bodies (see Dumke, 1991, pp.84–9).

Railways and industrialization

List called railway development the *Zollverein's* 'Siamese twin' and only major econometric surgery can separate the contribution of each to market integration. But whatever the debates on this score, there is unanimity amongst specialists that, excluding Belgium, the nineteenth-century economy in which railways gave the greatest incentive to industrial growth was Germany. By 1850, there were 6,000 kilometres of railway track (each requiring eighty-five tons of iron) in the German states, and a definite impact on the cost of bulk transport had already been registered; a further 21,000 kilometres were added between 1850 and 1875. Railway-building raised the demand for coal and iron products, provided orders for the most technologically progressive metal-working and machine-building firms, and encouraged them to draw up long-term investment programmes. Eleven of the twelve locomotives used on German railways in 1840 had been made in Britain; by 1850 only eleven of fifty-three had been imported. (Tilly, 1991, p.178 summarizes much of the literature.) Railways had a direct economic importance to state capital cities that became centres of construction, maintenance and repair: firms like Borsig and Pflug in Berlin, Maffei in Munich and Kessler in Karlsruhe were nuclei of engineering employment and machine-building .

Railways may have had a further importance in eroding some of the political prejudices against large-scale capitalist enterprise in states dominated by agrarian élites (which we encounter again below). One advantage of the mercantilist legacy was that it legitimized the state acting as an entrepreneur in the general interest. Government subsidies for railway building during the 1840s must be seen as contributing to 'the decisive break-through' in the expansion of industrial investment. Public financing of railway construction was proportionally more important outside Prussia, and in the German states overall accounted for about half of all railway capital funds up to 1850 (Tilly, 1978, pp.385, 415).

Financial institutions and industrialization

You will recall Gerschenkron's influential thesis that, in conditions of 'moderate' economic backwardness, industrial development was neces-sarily less reliant on autonomous market forces, and financial institutions (often with government support), had to mobilize investment capital that was not spontaneously forthcoming. Germany exemplified this pattern of substitution for Gerschenkron, with 'private' financial institutions as the major actors, and the state creating a benign environment.

There can be no doubt as to the financial institutions' industrial cre-ativity which was closely associated with the large-scale mobilization of capital through joint-stock companies, an aspect of industrialization so much more important in Germany than Britain or France (Kocka, 1978, p.539). The banking system expanded remarkably between 1848, when the first industrial investment bank was formed in Cologne, and 1857, when the financial crash brought investment to a juddering halt. A comprehen-sive structure of industrial credit was created, lifting the traditional restraints on the flow of capital to manufacturers. Joint-stock organization had originated in the need to limit risks for an individual investor, and the joint-stock investment banks carried the principle to a new level of sophis-tication by widening the pool of private investors and making these savings available for industry. The Pereire brothers were extremely adept in publi-cizing the idea with their *Crédit mobilier* (founded 1852), but the practice had already begun in Germany (and even earlier in Belgium). During the recovery from the 1857 crash, the banks re-asserted their role in industry and were particularly active in promoting companies and under-writing share issues during the hectic *Gründerjahre* (so called because of the num-ber of companies founded in these years) that followed unification.

Political fragmentation before 1870 meant that public authority had a variable role in creating the German capital market, and disunity was in itself something of an advantage because there was not a central bank imposing the same credit regime throughout the German states. But Prus-sia's traditionally close regulation of civil society was almost certainly an obstacle in the path of financial innovation. After the 1848 revolutions, economic liberals in the Prussian administration (such as the Finance Min-ister David Hansemann) saw a solution to the 'social question' and rural distress in the orderly growth of industrial employment. Capital for indus-trial enterprises was not easily forthcoming in Germany where investors preferred real estate and government bonds, so liberal bureaucrats advo-cated large low-interest loans for industry. Before leaving office Hansemann secured royal consent to a measure allowing the formation of joint-stock issuing banks that were to be controlled in part by the government. But the liberals had less political influence than conservative bureaucrats whose major policy goal was the preservation of an agrarian social hierarchy, and who favoured the flow of investment into the *Junker* estates of East Elbia. The Prussian government so restricted the formation of joint-stock banks, and so regulated their activities, that enterprising financiers set up new credit institutions *outside* Prussia where economic policy did not serve eastern agrarian interests. Thus Hesse-Darmstadt was chosen to host the first of the German credit banks – the *Darmstädter Bank* – that did so much to mobilize capital (including French foreign investment) for German industry during the 1850s. A judicious summary of Prussian economic policy in the reactionary years after 1848 suggests it was 'contradictory and fitful. The attitude of the government [to industrialization] was highly ambiguous, and this ambiguity was of itself a hindrance to the full development of Prussia's industrial potential' (Kitchen, 1978, p.94).

The giant corporation, finance capital and 'organized' capitalism

In the early twentieth century, when Marxists looked for the European 'model' of the capitalist future they found it in Germany in what they perceived as the dominance of finance over industrial capitalism and the creation of industrial monopolies in which business ownership was separated from the management of production. A new 'type' of power broker had emerged in the salaried entrepreneur, dedicated to corporate expansion for its own sake, and best exemplified by Emil Rathenau of the electrical giant Allgemeine Elektrizitäts Gesellschaft or AEG. The emergence of the giant corporation had a profound influence on the development of the advanced economies after 1900 and why Germany (along with the USA) should have pioneered this form of enterprise is a question we must address. But a word of caution: important though industrial giants were, their weight in the overall structure of business ownership and employment in 1914 should not be exaggerated. Small enterprises still flourished. In machine-making, for example, the average number of employers per firm in 1907 was twelve, and the small and middling firms in the industry actually employed *more* men at this time than in the early 1880s. What had changed over the years was the total labour force in machine-making had grown about four-fold and the *proportion* of workers employed by larger firms had rise from about a third to three-quarters (Clapham, 1936, 1968 edn, pp.287–8). The 'squeezing out' of small independent businessmen by competitive pressures was often very slow.

    So, why did industrial giants emerge, particularly in metallurgy, chemicals, electrical and heavy mechanical engineering? Market competition drove the *concentration* of capital forward, for entrepreneurs lowered their costs by investing in machines and plant, and by saving labour. To put it technically, the proportion of 'fixed' to 'variable' capital in their businesses rose. The fact that dynamic private enterprises (such as Siemens – originally a family firm) were generally compelled to convert to public companies in order to expand (and meet competition) reinforced a tendency to capital *centralization* because they became vulnerable to 'take over'. (Concentration takes place as individual enterprises grow by ploughing back profits; centralization when existing enterprises are combined in a single corporate ownership.) But why was the tendency to industrial concentration/centralization so strong in Germany around 1900 (and comparatively feeble in contemporary Britain and France)? The answer would seem to lie in the character of the industries in which Germany was outstandingly successful, and the support given to industry by financial institutions. We have already noted that success in the 'Second Industrial Revolution' depended on long-term investment in basic science, and you will have surmized that decades often elapsed between the patenting of a product and commercial exploitation. Only heavily capitalized firms backed by investors prepared to take the long view could succeed with, say, plastic derivatives of cellulose where the time-lag between discovery and marketing was exceptionally prolonged.

In our period, the electrical industry clearly demonstrates the interdependence of science and financial institutions in the growth of the giant industrial firm. The modern electrical industry was founded on the exploitation of the dynamo (invented in 1867 by Werner Siemens, 1816–92) – with the consequent breakthrough to electrical traction – and the telephone (adopted from the later 1870s). The German industry grew from statistical insignificance, in terms of employment, in the 1880s to a major sector by the early twentieth century as a result of the concentration of capital, patents – and state patronage – in two firms: Siemens and AEG. By 1907, AEG alone employed 31,000 workers. A syndicate of eight banks supported the company, while eleven acted for the rival Siemens group. The allocation of contracts for the electrification of urban transport by local and state governments also contributed handsomely to the firms' success by securing a basis of domestic business from which export drives into the world markets for cable and equipment were launched. These corporations expanded by taking over less successful rivals, but also by 'internalizing' functions hitherto left to other companies: world-wide sales and service organizations were created.

Generally speaking, internal growth funded by long-term capital was the most important factor in the creation of giant firms, but banks also underwrote company mergers that led to vertical integration and horizontal concentration. The financial institutions had rather distanced themselves from industry after the 1873 crash, but from the early 1890s co-operation between the banks and industrial concerns steadily increased. By 1913, financial and industrial capital was more deeply interpenetrated than in any other advanced economy: three-quarters of the balances of the major credit banks were made up of long-term loans to industrial customers. Additionally, as the scale of their loans, investments and share underwriting grew, so the banks sought direct influence on the production decisions of their clients and demanded representation on the 'supervisory boards' of the joint-stock companies they patronized. Bank directors became the largest single group among the members of the boards of industrial companies. It was not a one-way flow of power and influence, since leading industrialists were co-opted to the banks' boards. Nor were all industrial sectors equally penetrated by banking interests: in the coal and steel complex of the Rhine-Ruhr industrial region, the bankers really took the entrepreneurial initiative in creating vertical conglomerates. In the chemicals industry, by contrast, the bankers' role was more passive and the logic of the industrial processes dictated economies of scale which their capital merely facilitated. But by comparison with Britain or France, all of German industry was riddled with extensive financial connections that 'provided the banks with a comprehensive over-view of the entire industrial landscape, and thus a wider and safer arena for their own industrial promotions ... From their improved vantage point, the bankers adventured more confidently to acquire even larger blocks of industrial securities. And with these they were able to earn higher profits, pay higher dividends, and strengthen their own credit position'. (Trebilcock, 1981, p.95; see also Kocka, 1978, pp.565–70).

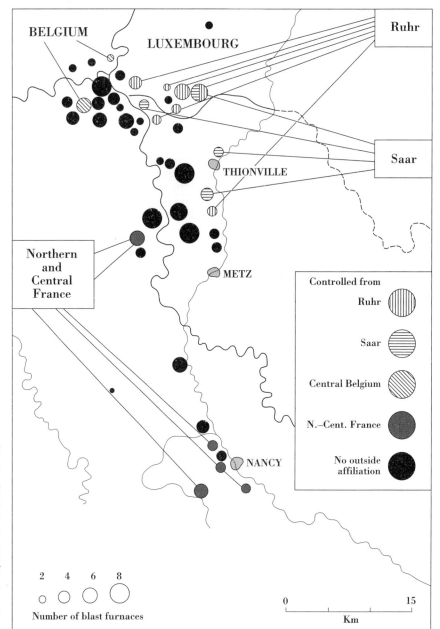

Figure 11
The European Steel
triangle, showing
ironworks on the Lorraine-
Luxembourg orefield and
their affiliation with iron
and steel companies
elsewhere in Western
Europe, c.1910. (From
N.J.G. Pounds, An
Historical Geography of
Europe 1800–1914,
Cambridge University
Press, Cambridge, 1985.)

Financial institutions had a further, long-lasting impact on the evolution of the German corporate capitalism by encouraging the cartelization of a vast range of production and marketing. By the early twentieth century, the productive capacity of industry was outstripping market demand in Germany, and business competition had generated more 'accentuated' cycles of boom and bust than was the case in France and Britain. Of course, individual firms (and their financial backers) gained from bankruptcies amongst their rivals, but to banks with financial interests in several firms in one industry there was more to be gained from 'organizing' the market than cut-throat competition. For this reason, they gave their backing to arrangements amongst producers that tended to maintain domestic prices artificially high while permitting export sales at a loss (i.e. 'dumping'). In states with stronger liberal traditions, cartels have frequently been adjudged conspiracies against the public, and outlawed, but the German legal climate was more benign and in 1897 the legality of cartels was confirmed by the Reich High Court. Cartelized production probably accounted for a quarter of total output in 1907. This proportion was far greater than in France and Britain, and the German agreements were much more stable. By the eve of the First World War, the co-operation between large industrial concerns for the control of product (and labour) markets, and the interdependence between industrial concerns and banks had set the German economy apart from its European rivals.

Nevertheless, the process of 'organizing' product markets by limiting competition was overlapping political boundaries by the early twentieth century. In the 'steel triangle' where France, Germany, Belgium and Luxembourg meet, firms were integrating across borders by investing in each other's businesses and entering agreements on prices, quotas and the exchange of output. Belgian producers and their associated financial institutions invested in the Lorraine ore mines, in the steel companies of Luxembourg and the Saar; German capital flowed into the Belgian steel industry, with the upshot that by 1914 about 17 per cent of share capital was accounted for by German holdings. The 'Europeanization' of this key industrial sector was already discernible forty or so years before it took institutional form in the European Coal and Steel Community.

Industrialization in the Tsarist Empire

The Tsarist empire was a multi-national state in which 'Great Russians' accounted for less than half the population, and Eastern Slavs (i.e. Ukrainians, 'White' Russians and Russians proper) just over two-thirds. The economic development of non-Russian regions in the nineteenth century was generally quite distinctive, partly because the abolition of serfdom came earlier and/or on different terms. In 1807, the French declared all equal before the law in the Duchy of Warsaw (which later formed part of the Congress Kingdom), and serfdom was abolished in the Baltic provinces in 1816–19, some forty-five years ahead of emancipation in the rest of the empire. These peripheral, non-Russian regions were amongst the most economically advanced (and consequently most urbanized) parts of the empire before the major industrialization drive of the 1890s. According to the 1897 census, the percentage of townspeople *(meshchane)* in Russian Poland was more than twice that of European Russia (23.5 as opposed to 10.65 per cent) (Shanin, 1985, p.62). (Note that there was a real distinction between 'townspeople' and 'town-dwellers', and the point is discussed further below.) The principal industrial concentration until 1880 was around the Dabrowa coal basin in Russian Poland where foreign entrepreneurs and craftsmen were encouraged to settle in the early nineteenth century. From the late 1830s, after Saxon businessmen had imported Belgian machinery, the town of Łódz became the

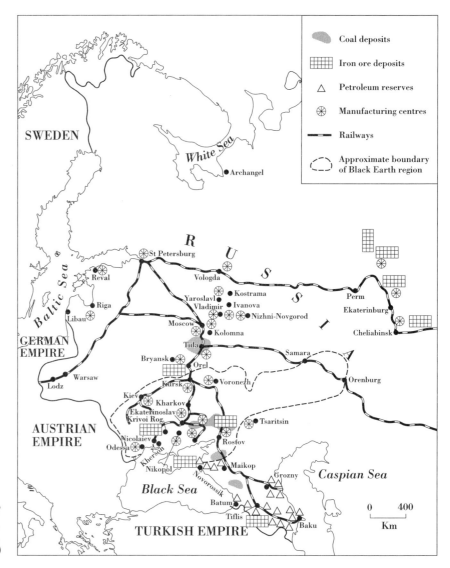

Figure 12
Russian industrial regions,
c.1900. (From Trebilcock,
1981.)

centre of a substantial textiles industry, acquiring a reputation as the 'Polish
Manchester'. After the Congress Kingdom was included in the Russian customs union in 1850, the cotton manufactures of Łódz gained easy access to the
Russian market. They benefited further from the imperial system when
restrictions were placed on the import of German goods in 1877. Industrial
production in Russian Poland increased tenfold between 1870 and 1890, and
continued to expand at a lower rate in the 1890s. 'Polish' industry was easily
supplied with fuel; its factories were to a large extent mechanized; organization of production and sales were first class; the common imperial market
compensated for the shortcomings of the 'Polish' market – two-thirds of production was sold in Russia. After 1890, 'Polish' growth slowed down, while
that of the rest of the empire accelerated, because the tariffs aimed at protect-
ing the infant industries of the Donets basin discriminated against semi-
manufactures and fuel imported overland into Russian Poland. The import

duties on, for example, rolled iron increased manufacturing costs to a point where foreigners were encouraged to 'jump over' the tariff wall and invest directly in 'Polish' iron-rolling.

We are mainly concerned with the fifty provinces of European Russia which contained three-quarters of the population and were a by-word for backwardness on the eve of serf emancipation in 1861. Though potentially the most powerful of the European states, Russia's military, administrative and technological inferiority had been exposed by the Crimean War. The French and British iron-clad steamers that swept the Black Sea of Russian vessels and the logistical railway laid down for their expeditionary forces manifested the new, industrial foundations of military power in Europe – foundations which the Tsarist empire clearly lacked. This had not been the case less than fifty years before. At the end of the eighteenth century, the world's largest iron industry was located in the Urals where abundant ore and charcoal, and seasonally navigable rivers, compensated for the huge distances from domestic and foreign markets. Much of the output was exported to Britain, though delivery normally required two years. During the Napoleonic wars, Russian artillery had not been technically inferior to the French and, in 1815, military prowess made the Tsar the arbiter of Europe. Was the aggrandisement of the patrimonial state achieved through the impoverishment of its people? Not according to recent scholars: during the eighteenth century, the average Russian had become better off and is now reckoned to have been little poorer than his/her British counterpart in 1807 when, according to Ian Blanchard, 'the two nations – Britain and Russia – stood at the very top of the European national-income league tables' (quoted in Crisp, 1991, p.251).

Up to the 1850s, the empire did keep pace with Continental rivals in some industrial sectors, notably mechanized cotton spinning which developed more rapidly in Russia than in the German states. However, comparative economic decline in a basic and militarily essential industry can be seen in Russia's falling proportion of world pig-iron output: from 12 per cent in 1830 to only 4 per cent in 1859. The empire now relied on imports for about a half of its basic metal requirements (Seton-Watson, 1967, p.244). In the short term, serf emancipation merely damaged the industrial structure by depriving the many enterprises worked by serfs of their labour. Liberated serfs at once took the opportunity of leaving the hated mines and factories: cast iron production in the Urals fell by a quarter between 1860 and 1862.

Exercise   To what would you attribute Russian backwardness? (Referring to your reading of the set book and parts of Unit 8 should help you answer this question.)

Discussion   The harshness and persistence of serfdom in the empire is – correctly – seen as a great obstacle to modern economic development. Serfs could not engage in certain key economic transactions – such as signing bills of exchange or offering mortgage securities – and even serfs who had left the land to work in the towns had to pay quitrents to their *pomeshchik* (lord) which constituted 'a tribute of industry to the serf-owners and a trammel upon industrial development' (Gerschenkron, 1966, pp.715, 719).

You may, however, have grasped that serfdom's retarding influence operated in a more complex way than is sometimes suggested. Without coerced serf labour, the Urals would not have been opened up to iron smelting in the first place and, until emancipated under Catherine II, a class of bonded industrial labourers had been attached with their families and descendants to the manufactories and mines in which they were employed. Serf entrepreneurs spearheaded the proto-industrialization of linen, leather and pottery manufacture, some of them amassing considerable fortunes while remaining bonded to their lords. Anderson (p.195) refers to Ludwig Knoop, the enterprising German who introduced British textile machinery; the first investors in such machines were rich peasant manufacturers, most of them only recently emancipated. Pipes even argues that 'Mechanical spinning of cotton yarn ... in Russia accommodated itself perfectly well to serfdom and indeed matured within its womb. The result of technological innovation was a peculiar blend of modern technology imported from the west and servile labour inherited from Muscovy, a mixture which contradicted the nineteenth-century belief that industrialism and bondage were incompatible'(Pipes, 1974, p.215).

This may overstate the case, but does suggest that serfdom retarded economic development *as much through its effects on agriculture as manufacturing.* All comparative studies confirm that rising agricultural productivity (if not an 'agricultural revolution') was a prerequisite for industrialization, since it furnished an investment surplus and enabled labour to be released to the secondary sector. Where the essence of serfdom was the provision of labour dues *(barshchina)* – which was the case in most of the 'Black Earth' belt – agricultural methods tended to be appallingly backward and wasteful because the decision-making landlord or his agent did not consider the peasant's time or labour as a cost. Elsewhere, servile dues had mostly been commuted to a money payment *(obrok)* and, though agriculture was less backward, the fact that the lord's income was not tied to economic services inhibited a calculating, 'market' mentality.

The serfs belonged to a legally designated hierarchy of feudal estates from which a bourgeoisie, such as had emerged in urban western Europe, was conspicuously absent. Until emancipation, Russian towns contained no free citizens in the European sense and had few economic functions. They were centres of administration or conspicuous consumption for the gentry where labour was withdrawn from productive work. Their inhabitants belonged to the rigidly limited merchant estate, unless they were nobles and officials, or their serfs. Pipes takes the absence of a bourgeoisie to have been the critical impediment to modern economic development, arguing that the 'second phase' of industrialism, beginning in the 1880s, found 'the middle class unprepared and unwilling'.

> Russia had missed the chance to create a bourgeoisie at a time when that had been possible, that is on the basis of [craft] manufacture and private capitalism; it was too late to do so in an age of mechanized industry dominated by joint-stock corporations and banks. Without experience in the simpler forms of capitalist finance and production, the Russian middle class lacked the capacity to participate in economic activity involving its more sophisticated forms. [Hence], the decisive role foreigners played [in the leading branches of heavy industry in the late nineteenth century]. (Pipes, 1974, p.218)

Furthermore, we must note that the autocracy and its advisers were not committed to industrialization before the 1880s, regarding its social corollary – the Godless proletariat – with fear and loathing. Before about 1850, key bureaucrats had similarly opposed railway development because it encouraged social egalitarianism and mobility, both inimical to Russia's agrarian system. Emancipation was conceived, not as a preliminary to industrial growth, but as a prophylaxis of peasant rebellion, a preventative step that would conserve the fundamentals of the agrarian order. In terms of economic development, the key measures of the reform era beginning in the 1850s were those imposing good-housekeeping on the bureaucracy and restricting its 'take' from the national product: state revenue and accounting procedures were carefully reviewed, and a unified budget of western type instituted.

The two phases of Russian industrialization before 1914

Table 8: The development of Industrial Production in Russia (in million poods; 1 pood=16.3 kilograms)

	1887	1890	1900	1908	1913
Pig-iron	36.1	54.8	176.8	171.1	283.0
Coal	276.2	366.5	986.4	1608.5	2215.0
Iron & Steel	35.5	48.3	163.0	147.5	246.5
Oil	155.0	226.0	631.1	528.6	561.3
Raw Cotton Inputs	11.5	8.3	16.0	21.2	25.9

Source: Portal, 1966

The data in Table 8 summarize well-known features of Russian industrial development between the late 1880s and the First World War. You will see that this was two-phased: the rate of increase in output was extraordinarily rapid during the 1890s, but at the turn of the century the industrial economy faced a crisis of overproduction that was then exacerbated by widespread rural disturbances, the uncertainties of the Russo-Japanese war and the revolutionary upheaval in its aftermath. In 1908, total industrial output was still below the 1900 level. In subsequent years, however, the industrial economy emerged from its prolonged depression and grew at rates close to those of the 1890s, bringing Russia to fifth place amongst the world's industrial powers by 1914.

The two phases of rapid growth had different characteristics: during the first, the directing intelligence behind state economic policy was S. Y. Witte (1849–1915) who brought to the Finance Ministry between 1892 and 1903 a vision of guided national economic development indebted to List. The economic boom in the 1890s was triggered off by an extensive programme of state-generated railway construction (the network doubled between 1886 and 1901) and the consequent large-scale demand for industrial goods. Although only 5 per cent of state expenditure went on railway development between 1880 and 1900, orders for rails and equipment were strategically placed to nourish Russian firms. The numbers employed in mechanical engineering rose two and half fold between 1890 and 1897. Social overhead capital took priority over social spending: expenditure by the Ministry of Communications rose from 26 millions in 1886 to 227 millions in 1897, that of the Ministry of Education from 21 million to 26 million roubles. A tariff wall was erected in 1891 to protect the infant industries of the central and southern regions, and free entry was allowed to only fourteen products for which there was little demand in Russia. From the late 1880s, the state raised investment capital abroad by floating guaranteed state loans, chiefly on the Paris Bourse. The French financial connection was reinforced by the 1894 diplomatic alliance and by monetary policies which strengthened the rouble and encouraged foreign investment in Russian joint-stock companies. By 1900 nearly half the share capital invested in Russian industry was foreign owned (Portal, 1966, p.825).

Discounting state bond-holding, most foreign investment was 'portfolio' share-holding effected through financial institutions. Nevertheless, Russian industrialization was also propelled forward by direct foreign investment: between 1888 and 1900, 253 foreign companies were set up in Russia, the majority (162) being Belgian mining and metallurgical enterprises, although the largest total capital was placed in the 54 French firms in the same sector (Seton-Watson, 1952, p.120). There were 38,042 industrial and mining enterprises in 1900, so in quantitative terms the foreign companies' presence was minuscule. But as importers of advanced technology and technical/managerial expertise, their qualitative significance was considerable. Tariffs facilitated, in particular, the exploitation of the coal and iron deposits of the Ukraine which more than any other region benefited from the inflow of foreign capital, attracted by the certainty of high profits safeguarded by regular orders from the state. In less than ten years, iron-making in the Urals was completely eclipsed by the newly arisen industrial complex linking the Donets coal field with the Krivoy Rog iron ores.

Why the delay before the industrialization drive of the 1890s? Why did it come as a 'great spurt' of capital-intensive growth? One, highly influential, answer to these questions lies in Gerschenkron's analysis of *agrarian policy* and industrialization in Tsarist Russia. In his view, it was the agrarian settlement of the 1860s which explains the paradox of a country 'so poor in capital and having much of its pre-accumulated wealth held in hands that would not make it available for industrial ventures, contriv[ing] to build up ... a modern industrial structure, many areas of which in technology and capital equipment compared favourably with those of economically advanced countries' (Gerschenkron, 1966, p.767). To summarize his argument: by contrast with the Prussian experience, emancipation failed to clear the decks for industrialization because it hampered the release of labour from the countryside and yet restricted the rural market for industrial products. The allotments of land under the Emancipation Edict were too small to generate the income needed for the high redemption payments and to extend the internal market for industrial commodities. Moreover, the edict created a land-owning peasantry rather than individual peasant landowners: households were secured on the land, and the proportion of agricultural wage labourers was tiny, but the vast majority of Great Russians were assigned to communes (*obshchinas*) which periodically re-distributed field strips amongst members and were held jointly responsible for their tax obligations. Without full property rights in their allotments, the peasants lacked an incentive to raise output by long-term investment. The traditionalism and inefficiency of peasant agriculture was preserved, if not reinforced, by emancipation. The political counterpart to the *obshchina* was the *mir* or local assembly in which were vested the police powers over the peasantry formerly exercised by the gentry. The agreement of the *mir*'s elected head was needed before a peasant could obtain an internal passport and leave the land to work in the towns, and it was normally withheld when redemption payments or tax arrears were outstanding. In addition to these restrictions on the flow of Russia's one abundant factor of production, labour, to industry, Gerschenkron discerned severe downward pressure on consumption in European Russia between 1879 and 1900 because of falling per capita output of wheat and rye, growing tax demands, and also an increased share of grain *exports* in total output under pressure of government policies. (A high level of exports was needed to sustain the international value of the rouble. An agrarian state importing real and financial capital on the scale of Russia in the 1880s and 1890s *had to* increase primary exports to settle its foreign trading balance. An imbalance of trade would have lowered the value of the rouble and made Russian assets unattractive to foreign investors.) A high rate of capital investment per worker in modern industry was essential to compensate for the inadequate labour supply and large-scale plants necessary so that the thin layer of managerial/technical personnel could be spread more widely. Growth based on skilled labour and family funds (as in France) can be slow and steady; but capital-intensive growth financed by foreign creditors has to be rapid to generate the profits that pay for equipment and provide dividends (Gerschenkron, 1966).

Not all of this account has stood the test of time. Territorial mobility was easier than Gerschenkron implied. True, 90 per cent of Russians were living in 1897 in the province in which they were born and the rate of growth of the urban population was slow by comparison with Germany or, say, the USA. But apart from seasonal workers, millions did migrate both to the cities and new areas of settlement. In 1897, some 69 per cent of St Peterburg's population and 74 per cent of Moscow's had been born outside the city boundaries (Shanin, 1985, p.64). Real wages in the capital's industries rose by an insignificant percentage between 1853–60 and 1910–13, which indicates that the urban sector was provided with all the unskilled labour required at a roughly constant wage. Agricultural production was less stagnant and rural consumption levels probably more buoyant than Gerschenkron concluded: it has been calculated that increasing grain production did match population growth, and that during 1850–1900, three-quarters of the increase in output in European Russia resulted from higher yields, only one-quarter from an expansion of the tilled area. Exports were not extracted from a desperate peasantry by fiscal pressure: the volume of crops retained by the peasants to feed their families and livestock rose as a proportion of net output in the late 1890s. The fact that the state treasury was able to shift the burden of tax revenue from direct to indirect taxes on items of common consumption (alcohol, tobacco and sugar) is evidence that consumption standards were at least maintained (peasants must have been buying these goods for the taxes to roll in). Furthermore, the structure and development of the industrial economy were rather less distinctive than Gerschenkron believed because he allowed the spectacular advances in the producers' goods industries to overshadow the longer-term and steadier growth in the consumer goods sector. Textiles, garment making and food processing employed a third of wage earners at the turn of the century, and whether measured in terms of employment or value of output the consumer industries as a whole easily outstripped the producers' goods industries.

Their origins pre-dated emancipation and their development was practically unaffected by the post-1900 slump. Similarly, the concentration of half Russia's factory labour in units of more than 1,000 workers led Gerschenkron to under-estimate the extent of workshop production in units of ten to fifteen hands, who often sub-contracted labour-intensive work from big firms at incredibly low rates. In 1900 there were in Moscow 190,000 'non-factory' small enterprise labourers as against 180,000 factory workers and in the provinces the predominance of 'non-factory' workers was overwhelming. Reflecting on these features of the industrial structure, Crisp dryly observes: 'It would seem that Russia's pattern of industrialization was not all that different from earlier industrializing economies ...' (Crisp, 1991, p.260; see also Gregory, 1991, pp.70–7).

During the second economic boom there were key changes in the pattern of industrial development. The role of the state as a customer of industry and a mobilizer of capital was much diminished, chiefly because the pace of railway development slackened (the mileage constructed between 1907 and 1911 was only a quarter of that between 1897 and 1901). With less government support, industry had to take the lead in organizing production and the market. Strong producers' cartels emerged in the metallurgical and minerals industries. The member firms of the most powerful, *Prodamet*, produced three-quarters of the empire's pig- and sheet-iron, and nearly half its rails. The syndicate distributed contracts according to quotas, and maintained high domestic prices. It had been formed in response to the crisis of over-production at the turn of the century, but by 1913 there was a universal complaint amongst industrial customers that its practices had created a chronic shortage of inputs. Linked to cartelization was a closer association between industry and the leading joint-stock banks which, to some extent, stepped into the vacuum left by the state. The banks' credit-creation policies and the entrepreneurial guidance they began to offer were, in Gerschenkron's terms, substitutes for the scarcity of capital and entrepreneurship in an economy that was now only 'moderately' backward. Indeed, from the point view of heavy industry 'Russia was at an advanced stage of evolution towards financial capitalism ... [with] ... the subordination of industrial business to banks, and the progressive formation of industrial and financial monopolies leading to trusts' (Portal, 1966, pp.849–50). There were, too, striking changes on the demand side of the economy with the growth of the mass consumers' market. The peasants' purchasing power improved with the rise in world wheat prices between 1906 and 1912, and they began to demand galvanized iron to roof their homes, as well as textiles, lighting oil, and agricultural implements. Additionally, the agrarian reforms of Interior Minister P.A. Stolypin (1862–1911) accelerated the movement to the towns and swelled the urban market. An increase in government social expenditure, on education in particular, improved the quality of the labour force and contributed to the changing pattern of demand.

The historical interpretation of the likely 'trajectory' of Russian social development in this period is a matter of fascinating speculation. Many, such as Gerschenkron, have 'surmise[d] that in the absence of war [in 1914] Russia would have continued on the road of progressive westernization' (Gerschenkron, 1962, reprinted in Emsley, 1979, p.207). But others, by no means all Marxists, have detected an escalating instability in an economy that combined the most advanced forms of capitalist industrialism with a backward peasant agriculture whose relative weight in the labour force remained stubbornly high because of rural over-population. We cannot know whether Russia would have avoided revolution, but *pace* Gerschenkron, we can specify ways the economy and society remained distinctly 'unwestern': the level of foreign investment was still extraordinarily high, and though probably declining as a proportion of total capital, it dominated leading industrial sectors. Foreign investments represented 90 per cent of the capital in mining, more than 40 per cent in metallurgy, and 50 per cent in chemicals (Portal, 1966, p.851). In this respect, the modern sector of the Russian economy was closer to the 'developing societies' of South America than Europe. Furthermore, the social structure of the major industrial centres demonstrated the failure to integrate workers into an urban culture comparable to western Europe's. Most urban wage earners were classified as peasants by 'social estate'. That this was not simply a formal designation is vividly illustrated by the fact that in Moscow, in 1908, some 46 per cent of printers were personally involved in part-time farming, just over half kept their families in the village and nearly 90 per cent regularly sent money to rural relatives (Shanin, 1985, p.118). Though Russia was no longer at the stage of economic backwardness where industrial development constantly threatens to outstrip a restricted market, the level of effective demand was dampened by low per capita incomes (about one-third of German on average) and by the relative self-sufficiency of peasant communities in which many consumer goods were still produced by craft methods.

Conclusion: do we have a typology for the study of European industrialization?

In this concluding section, I have taken a question posed by P. K. O'Brien because it returns us to the central problem of arranging the chronologies and diverse forms of European industrialization into patterns that illuminate both similarities and differences (O'Brien, 1986). O'Brien's question was prompted by widespread dissatisfaction amongst specialists with the typologies or 'models' used as research tools over the last four decades. They no longer appear satisfactory guidelines for future enquiry. The studies by Landes and Pollard that make *technological diffusion* the driving force behind a *single process* do not, O'Brien argues, take sufficient account of how technology was adapted to differences in resource endowments, domestic market structures, and opportunities in international trade.

Exercise   From your reading of this unit, do you find this objection well founded?

Discussion   I hope so. The French case demonstrates the need to qualify technological diffusionism and the concept of unitary process: the shortage of coal, but a comparative advantage in skilled labour and engineering expertise, together with the strong national demand for quality goods, all meant that industrialization in France was 'inflected' in distinct ways.

The French case also seems to me to discredit the close ally of the diffusionism, the *Rostow model* of industrialization. This, as you will recall, takes Britain as the 'paradigm' case and constructs a single pattern of industrialization from a stylized version of the 'First Industrial Revolution'. This procedure in itself has proved dubious because the stylization distorted empirical reality by exaggerating the speed with which industrialization took off and under-estimating the persistence of craft techniques and very small units of production in great swathes of the British economy beyond 1850. But this objection aside, France is now generally recognized as an 'early starter' whose industrialization neither replicated Britain's, nor exhibited the characteristics of industrial development in conditions of relative backwardness identified by Gerschenkron. With her 'balanced' social structure, France – not Britain – better typified a common pattern of European development during the nineteenth century; logic and the historical record suggest she was the paradigm case, and Britain a deviant offshore island. (An argument well made in Roehl, 1976.)

Gerschenkron's attempt to correlate specified features of industrialization with its timing and degrees of relative backwardness has provided a more robust typology. Nevertheless, research into Russian industrialization has revealed certain misconceptions about the weight of the capital goods sector, the role of the state, and the pace of change. To recapitulate, Russian industrialization originated (just as it did elsewhere) in the consumer goods industries and the capital goods sector was not as predominant as Gerschenkron believed. We have not looked at the role of the state at all closely, but revisionist work has shown a greater and more consistent concern for government revenue than for the formulation of something we would recognize as 'industrial policy'. Writing in the age of Keynes, Gerschenkron probably ascribed a more 'activist' role to the state than was conceivable by the official mind of late nineteenth-century Russia (or anywhere else in Europe). Research into a wider range of backward areas (particularly the Habsburg Empire, a fascinating case not discussed here) has underlined the empirical weaknesses of Gerschenkron's approach. What determined the pace and direction of industrialization in Hungary, for example, was not a strategy of 'substitutes', but natural resource endowment and trading opportunities afforded by the Empire's common market. One conclusion would appear to be that if 'patterns' of industrialization are discernible, they were determined by geology, geography and 'comparative advantage' in foreign trade.

O'Brien proposed that, in place of the familiar typologies, we accumulate and improve national statistics to evaluate better comparative advantage from trade data, and to make more scrupulous comparisons of per capita income, labour productivities, and the other indicators of comparative levels of economic development. For metaphors of 'take off' and 'big spurt', O'Brien would substitute the 'inductive statistical approach'. (We acquire knowledge 'inductively' when generalizations are revealed from the assembled facts.) Those students turned off by numbers – a good majority, I suspect – will find this a depressing conclusion. Certainly, we need better statistics, but I am not persuaded that O'Brien's proffered route out of the present typological confusion will be as rewarding as he thinks.

Exercise   From your reading of this unit, can you suggest why even 'improved' national statistics could still be very imperfect indicators of industrialization?

Discussion   National statistics are gross constructs that tell us about states and their aggregate populations, not regions and, as Pollard insists, the matrix of industrialization was regional. Crafts's re-working of the national statistics of British economic growth, though a signal contribution, does not reveal the regional specialization which was a fundamental feature of the process he analyses.

One conclusion we could draw is that our knowledge will be best advanced by comparative regional studies within and between national economies. Meanwhile, I think we still require bold, speculative generalizations – such as Rostow and Gerschenkron advanced – if only as preliminary mental 'maps' of Europe's industrial past. Simply by providing conceptual frameworks against which we can react, they help us select data and assess the significance of particular trends. If asked, in a TMA or exam, to *explain* the distinctive features of industrialization in conditions of economic backwardness, Gerschenkron's analytic framework would be the obvious starting-point. Numbers alone would not generate the explanation for which you were asked; a model or typology would have to figure somewhere.

References

Cameron, R. (1985), 'A new view of European industrialization', *Economic History Review*, 38, pp.1–23.

Clapham, J. (1936), *The Economic Development of France and Germany, 1815–1914*, Cambridge University Press, Cambridge. (First published 1921; revised edition reprinted 1968.)

Crafts, N.F.R. (1985), *British Economic Growth during the Industrial Revolution*, Oxford University Press, Oxford.

Crisp, O. (1991), 'Russia', in Sylla and Toniolo (eds).

Crouzet, F. (1974), 'French economic growth in the nineteenth century reconsidered', *History*, 59, pp.167–79.

Deane, P. and Cole, W. A. (1962), *British Economic Growth, 1688–1955*, Cambridge University Press, Cambridge.

Dumke, R. H. (1991), 'Tariffs and Market Structure: the German *Zollverein* as a model for economic integration'. in W. R. Lee (ed.), *German Industry and German Industrialisation*, Routledge, London.

Emsley, C. (ed.) (1979), *Conflict and Stability in Europe*, Croom Helm, London.

Fohlen, C. (1973), 'The Industrial Revolution in France, 1700–1914', in C. M. Cipolla, *The Fontana Economic History of Europe: Vol. IV, The Emergence of Industrial Societies*, Pt 1, Fontana, London.

Fohlen, C. (1978), 'Entrepreneurship and management in France in the nineteenth century', in *The Cambridge Economic History of Europe*: Vol VII, *The Industrial Economies: Capital, Labour and Enterprise*, Pt 1 *Britain, France, Germany and Scandinavia*, edited by P. Mathias and M.M. Postan, Cambridge University Press, Cambridge.

Gerschenkron, A. (1962), *Economic Backwardness in Historical Perspective*, Harvard University Press, Mass.

Gerschenkron, A. (1966) 'Agrarian policies and industrialization: Russia 1861–1917', in *The Cambridge Economic History of Europe*, Vol. VI, *The Industrial Revolutions and After: Incomes, Population and Technological Change* (II), edited by H. J. Habbakuk and M.M. Postan, Cambridge University Press, Cambridge.

Gregory, P. R. (1991), 'The role of the state in promoting economic development: the Russian case and its general implications', in Sylla and Toniolo (eds).

Kitchen, M. (1978), *The Political Economy of Germany, 1815–1914*, Croom Helm, London.

Kocka, J. (1978) 'Entrepreneurs and managers in German industrialization' in *The Cambridge Economic History of Europe*: Vol VII, *The Industrial Economies: Capital, Labour and Enterprise*, Pt 1 *Britain, France, Germany and Scandinavia*, edited by P. Mathias and M.M. Postan, Cambridge University Press, Cambridge.

Landes, D. (1969), *Technological Change and Industrial Development in Western Europe from 1750 to the Present*, Cambridge University Press, Cambridge.

Lee, W. R. (ed.) (1991), *German Industry and German Industrialisation*, Routledge, London.

Léon, P. (1976), 'Le moteur de l'industrialisation, l'entreprise industrielle', in *Histoire économique et sociale de la France*, vol.3–2, *L'Avènement de l'ère industrielle*, dir. E. Labrousse, sous la direction de F. Braudel, PUF.

Lévy-Leboyer M. (1968), 'Les Processus de l'industrialisation: cas de l'Angleterre et de la France', *Revue Historique*, 239, pp.281–98.

Lévy-Leboyer M. (1978), 'Capital investment and economic growth in France, 1820–1930', in *The Cambridge Economic History of Europe*: Vol VII, *The Industrial Economies: Capital, Labour and Enterprise*, Pt 1 *Britain, France, Germany and Scandinavia*, edited by P. Mathias and M. M. Postan, Cambridge University Press, Cambridge.

Lilley S. (1973), 'Technological progress and the Industrial Revolution', in C. M. Cipolla (ed.), *The Fontana Economic History of Europe*, Vol III, *The Industrial Revolution*, Fontana, London.

Marczewski J. (1963), 'The Take-off Hypothesis and French Experience', in W. W. Rostow (ed.), *The Economics of Take-off into Sustained Growth*, Macmillan, London.

Mathias, P. (1969), *The First Industrial Nation*, Methuen, London.

Mathias, P. and Postan, M. M. (eds) (1978), *The Cambridge Economic History of Europe*: Vol VII, *The Industrial Economies: Capital, Labour and Enterprise*, Pt 1 *Britain, France, Germany and Scandinavia*, Cambridge University Press, Cambridge.

Milward, A. S. and Saul, B. (1973), *The Economic Development of Continental Europe, 1780 –1870*, Allen and Unwin, London.

Milward, A. S. and Saul, B. (1977), *The Development of the Economies of Continental Europe, 1850–1914*, Allen and Unwin, London.

Mitchell, B. R. (1992), *International Historical Statistics: Europe 1750–1988*, Macmillan, London.

O'Brien, P. K. (1986), 'Do we have a typology for the study of European industrialization in the XIXth century?', *Journal of European Economic History*, 15, 2, pp.291–333.

O'Brien, P. K. (1993) 'Introduction: modern conceptions of the Industrial Revolution', in P.K. O'Brien and R. Quinault (eds).

O'Brien, P. K. and Keyder, C. (1978), *Economic Growth in France and Britain, 1780–1914: two paths to the twentieth century*, Allen and Unwin, London.

O'Brien P. K., and Quinault, R. (eds) (1993), *The Industrial Revolution and British Society*, Cambridge University Press, Cambridge.

Pipes, R. (1974), *Russia under the Old Regime*, Weidenfeld, London.

Pollard, S. (1981), *Peaceful Conquest: the Industrialization of Europe 1760–1970*, Oxford University Press, Oxford.

Portal, R. (1966), 'The Industrialization of Russia', in *The Cambridge Economic History of Europe*, Vol. VI, *The Industrial Revolutions and After: Incomes, Population and Technological Change* (II), edited by H. J. Habbakuk and M.M. Postan, Cambridge University Press, Cambridge.

Roehl, R. (1976), 'French Industrialization: A Reconsideration', *Explorations in Economic History*, 13, pp.233–81.

Rostow, W. W. (1960), *The Stages of Economic Growth*, Cambridge University Press, Cambridge.

Rostow, W. W. (1978), *The World Economy: History and Prospect*, Macmillan, London.

Seton-Watson, H. (1952), *The Decline of Imperial Russia 1855–1914*, Methuen, London.

Seton-Watson, H. (1967), *The Russian Empire, 1801–1917*, Oxford University Press, Oxford.

Shanin, T. (1985), *Russia as a 'Developing Society': Vol.1 The Roots of Otherness: Russia's Turn of Century*, Macmillan, London.

Sheehan, J. J. (1989), *German History 1770–1866*, Oxford University Press, Oxford.

Stearns, P. N. (1975), *Lives of Labour: Work in a Maturing Industrial Society*, Croom Helm, London.

Sylla, R. and Toniolo, G. (eds) (1991), *Patterns of European Industrialization*, Routledge, London.

Tilly, R. (1978), 'Capital formation in Germany in the nineteenth century', *The Cambridge Economic History of Europe*: Vol VII, *The Industrial Economies: Capital, Labour and Enterprise*, Pt 1 *Britain, France, Germany and Scandinavia*, edited by P. Mathias and M.M. Postan, Cambridge University Press, Cambridge.

Tilly, R. (1991), 'Germany', in Sylla and Toniolo (eds).

Trebilcock, C. (1981), *The Industrialization of the Continental Powers 1780–1914*, Longman, London.

Unit 10
The development of the European international economy up to 1914

Prepared for the course team by Bernard Waites

Contents

Study timetable

Weeks of Study	Texts	Video	AC
1	Unit 10	Video 2	

Aims
The aim of the unit is to describe and analyse the international economy of nineteenth-century Europe.

Objectives
By the end of the unit you should be able to understand:

1   the system of foreign trade and international financing which by the 1900s linked the European states into mutual economic dependence;

2   Europe's dominant position in the world trading economy.

Introduction

By any yardstick we choose, the century between Waterloo and 1914 was exceptionally important for the growth of foreign trade: Europe's external trade probably grew three or four times in the eighteenth century; between 1830 and 1913, it grew about sixteenfold in current values. Because export prices fell very rapidly after 1830, the growth in the volume of trade was even greater; growth achieved during 1850–73 was not to be matched until the post-Second World War boom. Another yardstick we can take is the percentage of GNP exported: the best guess is that in 1815 it can have been no more than three per cent for Europe as a whole (which I will take to include all of Russia, but to exclude all the Ottoman Empire). In 1913, Europe's overall export rate was about 14 per cent, though it varied greatly according to the size of the different national economies and their levels of development. Again, this export rate was unmatched until recent years. In other words, the importance of external trade relative to total economic activity in Europe has rarely been greater than at the end of the nineteenth, beginning of the twentieth century. If trade has ever been 'an engine of growth', it must have been during our period.

With respect to foreign investment we can be still more emphatic: never has external lending by the world's major creditor nations accounted for such a large share of national product as it did in later nineteenth- and early twentieth-century Europe. A historical comparison will bring this home to you: during the Marshall Plan years, the American administration mobilized about three per cent of US GNP per year to rebuild the shattered economies of post-war western Europe, proportionately the largest overseas investment effort by a national economy in recent times. In the decade before 1914, British private investors routinely mobilized eight per cent of UK GNP per year to invest overseas. Never before, or since, has one nation committed so much of its national income and savings to capital formation in other economies (Edelstein, 1981, p.70). I must emphasize that British investors were not alone in finding foreign outlets for their savings so attractive: the French level of foreign investment was also exceptionally high by historical standards, and German foreign investments were rising before the First World War. Can this surge of capital exports be related to European political expansion in the less developed world, as theorists of imperialism have claimed ever since? Space precludes a full discussion of that question, but by looking at the location and different types of foreign investment favoured by British and Continental European savers, we can throw some light on it.

European international trade

Here, we will analyse the growth, direction, and commodity composition of European international trade between 1815 (or more particularly 1830 when trade statistics become more reliable) and 1913. First a few words of definition: any trade across political frontiers is international (or 'foreign' or 'external'), and we can distinguish between *intra-* and *extra-European* trade. The distinction is crucial when comparing the pattern of Britain's trade with that of other European states. From the point of view of an

exporting country, home-produced exports are its *special* trade and our
main concern here. The re-exporting of colonial commodities was a significant proportion of British (and Dutch) commerce up to the mid-nineteenth
century, but became much less so after the abolition of *mercantilist* restrictions opened up the British empire to *multilateral* world trade.
('Mercantilism' refers to the state regulation of trade in order to secure
commercial advantages for one's nationals. Such regulations had been particularly stringent under the 'old' colonial system when carriers from the
European metropoles had the exclusive right of trade with their colonies.
Britain first liberalized and then, with the abrogation of the Navigation
Laws in 1849, abolished this restrictive system. One consequence was that
later nineteenth-century India engaged in multilateral – or 'many-sided' –
trade: she became the largest market for British manufactures, but found
outlets for her own surpluses of primary products and semi-manufactures
in Japan, China, the United States and Continental Europe.)

The tables you will consider have been drawn from Paul Bairoch's
*Commerce extérieur et développement économique de l'Europe au XIXe
siècle* (1976), partly because sticking to one source ensures internal consist-
ency, but chiefly because his data are thought the best approximations in the
field. All values are expressed in current 'Gold Standard' dollars. (Between
1879 and 1914, when the Gold Standard prevailed amongst the major cur-
rencies, the £ sterling was equivalent to $4.8665. The exchange rate was
remarkably stable in this period.) The figures themselves are less important
than the underlying economic trends, and the relative positions of the different national economies, indicated by them. The tables are *not* primary
sources, and often involve imputing global totals from fragmentary data.
Where, for example, no complete record of all European trade exists, the global amount has to be arrived at by assuming that the imports and exports of
major trading nations such as Britain (whose commercial statistics go back to
the seventeenth century) represented a certain proportion of the whole.

Table 1 puts nineteenth-century European trade into a global context. The figures for the beginning of the century are *very* speculative, but
the general conclusion that Europe's share of world exports was disproportionate to its share of world population and world GNP is universally
accepted. Despite the intercontinental migration of around 46 million
Europeans between 1815 and 1915 (more than four-fifths left after 1865),
Europe increased its share of world population and, by a much greater
margin, world GNP. Its share of exports fell as other regions (such as
South America) entered international trade.

Table 1: Europe's share of world exports, 1800–1910 (in millions of current $)

Exports	1800	1860	1880	1900	1910
World	990	3,220	6,370	9,210	14,810
Europe	660	2,100	4,050	5,480	8,650
European %	66.7	65.2	63.6	59.5	58.4
Europe's share of world GNP and population (in %s)					
Population	21.0	23.3	25.1	26.0	26.5
GNP	26.1	35.6	39.9	42.6	42.4

Source: Bairoch, 1976, p.18.

Table 2 presents a more detailed picture of the growth of European exports in current values after 1830. The fourth column, showing the export price index, indicates a volume increase in exports greater than the increase in value. The index reflects the general price deflation during the nineteenth century, and the sharp upward inflation before the First World War.

Table 2: Growth of European exports (in millions of current $)

Year	GNP	Exports	As % of GNP	Price index[†]
1830	14,660*	645*	4.4*	157*
1860	22,370	2,105	9.4	137
1890	36,730	4,630	12.6	105
1913	75,160	10,550	14.0	111
1970	1,372,000	169,100	12.3	n/a

Source: Bairoch, 1976, pp.20, 65.
(*indicates a considerably larger margin of error than the other figures
[†] 1900 = 100)

Table 3 shows the percentage share in total European exports of Europe's major trading economies between 1830 and 1910 (each year in the Table represents a triennial average to even out the effects of annual fluctuations). As you will see, Britain was the major trading nation throughout the period, but the apogee of its commercial pre-eminence was reached around the 1860s. France ceded its position as the second large exporter to Germany, which by the First World War was threatening Britain's supremacy: Germany accounted for 23 per cent of European exports in 1913, Britain for 24 per cent. The three largest western European economies were all exporting roughly the same proportion of their GNP by 1910: for Britain, the figure was 17.5 per cent, for France 15.3 per cent, and for Germany 14.6 per cent. The territorially largest states, Russia and Austria-Hungary, each exported only 6 to 7 per cent of their national product. There was a positive correlation between the export ratio and the level of development, but a negative one with the size of the economy in question. Belgium exported 35.5 per cent of its national product, and Denmark and Switzerland each about a quarter.

Table 3: Percentage shares of European exports of the major trading economies

	1830	1860	1880	1890	1900	1910
Germany	n/a	18.4	18.2	17.4	19.6	20.4
Belgium	2.9	4.0	5.9	6.1	6.7	7.3
France	15.9	19.2	16.3	15.3	14.4	13.4
UK	27.5	29.8	26.0	26.6	24.7	23.7
Russia	7.9	5.6	6.7	8.3	6.6	8.9
Austria-Hungary	4.7	5.8	7.4	6.5	7.0	5.6

Source: Bairoch, 1976, p.77.

Table 4 Geographical structure of European exports – % of total exports

Year	Europe	N. America	S. America	Asia	Africa	Oceania
1860	67.5	9.1	7.7	10.0	3.2	2.5
1880	72.2	8.4	6.0	8.6	2.5	2.3
1990	71.1	6.7	5.3	9.8	4.4	2.7
1910	67.8	7.6	7.5	9.8	4.8	2.4

Source: Bairoch, 1976, p.82.

Table 5: Growth of total European imports (in millions of current $)

1860	2,373					
1880	5,078					
1900	6,913					
1910	10,462					
Geographical origins of European imports – % of total imports						
Year	Europe	N. America	S. America	Asia	Africa	Oceania
1860	61.0	14.3	7.8	12.1	3.2	1.7
1880	64.7	16.2	6.1	8.1	2.7	2.2
1900	60.7	18.4	6.5	8.6	3.1	2.7
1910	60.0	14.0	8.2	10.0	4.5	3.4

Source: Bairoch, 1976, p.84.

Exercise   Tables 4 and 5 (above), enable us to see where Europe's exports were going and where its imports were coming from in the later nineteenth- and early twentieth-century. What do they tell us about the relative importance of intra-European and extra-European trade, and Europe's trading balance with the rest of the world?

Discussion   Intra-European trade was always much more important for Europe than extra-European. The European states absorbed well over two-thirds of each other's exports throughout the period, and furnished about three-fifths of European imports. But you will have noticed the consistent discrepancy between the two, and this indicates the considerable trading imbalance in extra-European, more precisely North American trade. North America was the single most important overseas market for European goods during the first half of the nineteenth century, but thereafter American manufacturers were able to substitute for imports behind tariff barriers, and the unprotected Asian economies absorbed a larger proportion of extra-European exports. However, North Americans continued to be the most important suppliers of cotton, the industrial crop in greatest demand in Europe, and exported increasing quantities of wheat from the 1870s. Hence their dominant position in the import figures.

Now let us look more closely at changes in the *rate of growth* in the volume of European exports. Annual trade statistics show sharp fluctuations due to poor harvests and 'exogenous' events, such as the American Civil War. Underlying these fluctuations, however, were definite phases of accelerated and decelerated growth. What caused these periodic changes of 'pace' is clearly of great interest.

Table 6: The growth in the rate of European exports by volume – average annual percentages

1815–1846/7	3.5–4%
1847/9–1872	5.5–6%
1873–1894/5	2.1%
1897–1913	4.1%

Exercise   Look at Table 6 and see if you can suggest why there was a particularly rapid phase of growth of European exports in the third quarter of the nineteenth century, followed by two decades when the growth rate was comparatively sluggish. (For those who have forgotten the implications of compound growth rates, let me remind you that £100 growing at the rate of 6 per cent a year will reach £201.22 over 12 years; at 2 per cent a year, it will reach £126.80 in the same period.)

Discussion   My guess is that you will have associated changes in the growth rate of trade with changes in the tariff policies of the major trading nations, and correlated 'free trade' with rapid growth and sluggish growth with the return to protection. Well, it shows you're thinking, but the answer is only partially correct and more wrong than right.

The beginning, around 1848, of the phase of rapid growth was so close to the liberalization of the British economy with the abolition of the Corn Laws in 1846, the Navigation Acts, and (by 1853) of import duties on nearly all manufactured articles that a causal relationship is undeniable. Britain became an open market for French and German goods, yet during the 1850s nearly doubled its own exports. The success of the British economy in these years inspired the European free trade movement. The French economist, Michel Chevalier (1806–79) wrote in 1852:

> Britain's adoption of the principle of the freedom of trade is one of the great events of the century. When such a powerful and enlightened nation not only puts such a great principle into practice but is well known to have profited by it, how can its emulators fail to follow the same way? (cited in Bairoch, 1989, p.30)

As a member of Napoleon III's Council of State, Chevalier signed, with Richard Cobden (1804–65) the Anglo-French treaty of 1860 that inaugurated the liberalization of trade over much of Europe. Trade was never completely 'free': in 1875, by when the major trading states had signed the network of 'Cobden' treaties according each other 'most favoured nation status', the level of import duties on manufactures on the Continent averaged 9–12 per cent according to value, with a range from 5 per cent in Germany, to 12–15 per cent in France and 15–20 per cent in Russia and Austria-Hungary. The fiscal barriers were not insignificant, but were never so low as between 1860 and *c.*1879.

But, apart from trade liberalization, there were other causal factors operating simultaneously. For many bulky goods, the decline in *transport costs* from the late 1840s had a proportionally greater impact on final import prices than tariff reductions, which generally came when the trade boom was already in full swing. Between 1840–5 and 1870–5, there was a fourfold decline in the average costs of land transport in real terms, while the speed with which freight moved increased tenfold. Falling transport costs alone would have accounted for a 30 per cent drop in the price of imported wheat (Bairoch, 1989, p.24, p.56).

Though the real cost of maritime freight charges did not fall quite so rapidly, the period when the greatest productivity gains were made in both land and sea transport more or less coincided with the great trade boom. A further factor in this boom was the fortuitous injection of liquid cash into the world money supply following the Californian and Australian gold discoveries. Lastly, but not least, the rapid growth in British domestic production and incomes between 1850 and 1873 expanded international markets to a degree unmatched in any other advanced economy of the time. As early as 1860, total British imports were equal to 30 per cent of net national income (calculated from Mitchell and Deane, 1962, pp.267, 283). Allowing for re-exports, we can say for every £4 spent in Britain, £1 went on imported goods.

A compelling reason for thinking that tariffs played only a small part in determining the growth rate of trade is that its deceleration began before the world economic crisis of 1873, and at a time when tariff policies were very liberal. The return to protection, whose beginnings can be dated approximately to the German tariff of 1879, was a *response to*, and not a cause of the trade slump. So what caused the trade slump? Why was free trade so benign a condition for the British economy during the 1850s and 1860s, yet apparently so adverse a condition for the Continental economies during the 1870s? The answer would appear to lie in the impact of North American grain imports on the agrarian sectors of the European economies which, you will recall, were proportionally much larger in terms of their labour force in 1880 than Britain's agriculture had been in 1840.

Once transport costs had fallen, Europe's grain farmers simply could not compete with the mid-West prairies, where mechanized reaping on abundant fertile land led to soaring output and labour productivity. Imports of North American cereals were only a quarter of a million tons a year during the 1850s, but reached 2.14 m. tons by the early 1870s. Except in Britain, imports provided a fairly modest proportion of total requirements (about a fifth in Germany on the eve of the 1879 tariff), but it was enough to drive down the market price of European cereals, and hence farm income. Farming families were such a large proportion of the population that the stagnation of their purchasing power outweighed the increase in the disposable income of urban workers due to lower food prices. Such, in brief, was the cause of the structural crisis affecting the late nineteenth-century European economies, a crisis reflected in the down turn of cross-border trade no less than a slower growth in production.

The relatively minor role of tariffs (at least, at the levels actually adopted) would appear to be confirmed by the resurgence of economic growth, and international trade, in Continental Europe from 1895. This was *after* the general return to protection which, though initiated in the late 1870s, was a piecemeal process whose full, cumulative effects were not felt until the early 1890s. (By coincidence, many liberal commercial treaties lapsed in 1892 when France introduced the Méline tariff.)

The fastest growing economies, with the most rapidly expanding exports, were amongst the most protected, while the slowest growing between the late 1890s and 1914 was free-trading Britain whose share of European exports fell. To imply that tariffs were 'good' for trade would be absurd; evidently, however, protection did not greatly inhibit it. This was because trade was dependent fundamentally on economic growth, and not vice versa.

The return to a high growth rate in European trade was principally due to Germany's spectacular industrial expansion and concomitant urbanization: by 1890, she accounted for a larger share of *intra*-European trade than Britain, and in a few years her industrial economy had reached the critical mass that allowed it to function as the flywheel of renewed European growth. Imports of raw materials and food were sucked in while surpluses of manufactures were created that could, if necessary, be 'dumped' abroad. Tariffs were simply part of the cost the urban classes paid to ease the transition of agrarian producers (in Germany and elsewhere) to industrialism. The level of duty on grain was about twice that on manufactured imports (36 per cent as opposed to 17 per cent in Germany in 1913), and the effect was to restrict (though far from completely) German consumers' access to the agrarian resources of the extra-European world, especially by comparison with their British counterparts. To illustrate: exports from the Argentine to Germany rose more than a two and a half times between 1900 and 1913, but to Britain they rose over five times. In Britain's case, Argentine imports were principally wheat, in Germany meat. Germany, unlike Britain, strengthened her commercial ties with the agrarian economies of central and eastern Europe. Commercial treaties with Austria-Hungary (1891) and Russia allowed for reduced duties on grain imports from these countries and easier entry for German manufactures.

Table 7: Comparison of the geographic structures of British and Continental European trade – %s of totals

Year		Europe	N.America	S. America	Asia	Africa	Oceania
Exports 1860	UK	34.3	16.6	12.0	25.7	3.2	8.2
	Con Europe	82.0	5.8	5.8	3.1	3.2	0.1
1880	UK	35.6	15.9	10.2	25.4	4.3	8.4
	Con Europe	85.0	5.8	4.5	2.8	1.8	0.1
1910	UK	35.2	11.6	12.6	24.5	7.4	8.6
	Con Europe	78.0	6.4	5.9	5.2	3.9	0.5
Imports 1860	UK	31.0	26.7	10.1	23.2	4.5	4.5
	Con Europe	77.5	7.4	6.6	6.0	2.5	0.1
1880	UK	41.4	30.9	6.1	12.0	3.7	5.9
	Con Europe	75.5	9.5	6.0	6.3	2.2	0.4
1910	UK	45.1	23.8	9.1	10.3	4.8	6.9
	Con Europe	65.2	10.5	8.0	9.8	4.4	2.1

Source: Bairoch, 1976, p.88.

Exercise   The discussion has taken us slightly ahead of ourselves, and I would now like you to revert to the more general picture by comparing the geographic structures of British and Continental European trade over time. What sharp differences are revealed by Table 7?

Discussion   Unlike that of Continental Europe, Britain's export trade was geographically dispersed in the wider world. Only about a fifth of continental Europe's exports entered inter-continental trade; for Britain it was about two-thirds. Colonies of British settlement – as in Oceania – absorbed a share of British exports disproportionate to their populations. (Notice that in 1880, twice as many British goods were sold to the markets of Australia and New Zealand than the entire continent of Africa.) Overall, the geographical structure of exports was very stable. With respect to imports, the picture is significantly different: Britain became much more reliant on imports from Continental Europe, and Europeans more dependent on imports from the wider world over the period.

Table 8: Product structure of European commerce – in %s of the total (Annual figures represent three or four-year averages)

Year	Exports		Imports	
	Manufactures	Primary Products	Manu's	P P'cts
1830	63.5	36.5	11.5	88.5
1860	60.5	39.5	9.5	90.5
1893	55.2	44.7	20.1	79.9
1912	55.7	44.3	22.6	77.4

Source: Bairoch, 1976, p.92.

Table 9: Commodity structure of European exports in 1913 – %s of total exports of major commercial powers

	Germany	France	UK
Primary products	28.4	36.6	20.6
Foodstuffs	11.0	15.6	6.9
Raw Materials	17.4	21.0	13.7
Manufactures	71.6	63.4	79.4
Metals	16.1	5.6	13.1
Machines	9.8	2.0	7.9
Vehicles	2.3	4.3	4.7
Chemicals	8.0	4.2	4.0
Textiles	13.2	24.9	38.3
Others	22.2	22.3	11.4
Total	100	100	100

Source: Bairoch, 1976, p.94.

Exercise   Let us now turn to the commodity structure of European trade: how would you explain the changing proportions of manufactures and primary products in European imports and exports revealed in Table 8? One nation's exports are another's imports, so one might have thought the proportions in the *Exports* and *Imports* columns would 'fit'; why are they so discrepant? Table 9 allows you to compare the export commodity structure of the major European trading economies in 1913. What were the main differences in the export schedules of Britain, Germany and France?

Discussion   Like me, you may have been puzzled by the steady decline in the proportion of manufactures in European *exports* over the period, given that industrialization was transforming the European economies. But bear in mind that the reallocation of the work force to manufacturing usually created food deficits, while demand for fuel, timber and other raw materials rose. The value of the primary imports 'sucked in' by the advancing economies was normally greater than their exports of manufactures. Recall, too, the preponderance of intra-European trade in Europe's external trade: falling transport costs often favoured an international division of labour between the primary and secondary sectors of neighbouring states (e.g. Germany and Austria-Hungary) and promoted 'complementary' trades between regions with natural resource deficiencies (thus France had a chronic coal deficit but, from around 1880, an exportable surplus of iron ore).

The fact that the proportions in the two columns don't fit is due to the great preponderance of primary products in the imports from the wider world.

Table 9 makes evident the larger proportion of primary products in German, but more especially, French exports as compared with Britain, as well as the strong concentration of British exports on textiles. Britain exported £127 m. worth of cotton goods in 1913 – easily the single most valuable item; next came iron and steel (£55m.) and coal (£54 m.). Imports of raw cotton (£70.6 m.) ranked second after imports of grain and flour (£80.9 m.); third came meat and animals (£56.7 m.) (figures from Mitchell and Deane, 1962, p.300).

The changing terms of trade

In the analysis of international exchange, the terms of trade – by which we mean *export prices relative to import prices* – are more significant than absolute price increases or decreases. We can follow the movement in *Britain's* barter terms of trade by comparing the weighted index for average export prices (which are always quoted 'free on board' – f.o.b.) with the index for average import prices (which include freight and insurance charges – c.i.f.)

Table 10: British terms of trade in the nineteenth century

	Index of average export prices	Index of average import prices
1820	234.8	150
1840	128.5	122.3
1860	110.6	116
1880	100	100
1900	91.7	76.4
1913	96.9	83.4

Source: Imlah, 1958, p.86.

Exercise   Look at the indices in Table 10, summarize the trends between 1820 and 1913 (1880 = 100), and see if you can suggest any explanation for them.

Discussion   Export prices fell proportionally much more than import prices between 1820 and 1880 and this represented a considerable deterioration in Britain's barter terms of trade. Most of the fall took place by 1860 and the reason is not hard to seek: exports were predominantly manufactures, and the productivity gains of mechanization led to falling prices for cottons and other mass-produced goods. One hundred yards of Lancashire cloth would exchange for a lot less Portuguese wine in 1860 than it did in 1820. Of course, income from trade rose much more in Lancashire than in Portugal in these decades because the total amount of cloth produced and exported increased hugely, while wine-making technique remained much as it had been for centuries. After 1880, the trend was reversed: British export prices rose faster than import prices, so barter terms of trade improved.

The explanation for this post-1880 movement is more problematic: certainly, British consumers of wheat and other primary imports were benefiting from the productivity gains made by American prairie farmers and other agricultural producers of temperate products. But note that the prices compared by our indices are not the same: imports include freight costs, and as a rule these represent a much higher proportion of the value of 'bulk' goods (grain, raw materials, etc.) than they do of manufactures. (Transport costs for a thousand tons of baled, raw cotton were much the same as for a thousand tons of cotton piece goods in 1880, but the value of the cotton goods was far greater.) The price of food and raw material imports into Britain continued to fall after 1880 partly because productivity gains in inter-continental transport were still being made.

In the video interview, Clive Trebilcock echoes a widespread belief (almost an article of faith) that primary producers' terms of trade deteriorated over the long term. This is challengeable. Looking at Britain's terms of trade – which are a reasonable proxy for the exchange of European manufacturers for primary imports from the wider world – it is easy to assume that because they improved after 1880 then the terms of trade of primary exporters to Britain must have deteriorated. But this assumption is undermined once we take the differential impact of falling transport costs into account. Primary exporters' terms of trade were *not* a reciprocal of Britain's, and need to be calculated for individual commodities since demand conditions in the industrialized countries for different products varied greatly. (There was falling demand for cane sugar, for example, but rising demand for rubber.) For eleven key tropical commodities between 1880 and 1913, the terms of trade fell in four cases, but rose in six and were constant in one case (reported in Hanson, 1980, p.120). Generalizations are obviously hazardous, and I would not want to substitute one article of faith for another. But it is worth pointing out that Bairoch has produced data to show that average export prices for primary products relative to export prices of manufactures actually improved by 20 to 40 per cent between 1870 and 1929 (Bairoch, 1975, pp.111–13).

The 'gains' of trade

We tend to assume that international trade is a 'good thing' without stopping to consider that, economically, it has little to commend it. The end of production is consumption, and exporting goods simply denies them to the domestic consumer while imposing higher than usual transport and transaction costs on foreign customers. The benefit of a country's exports lies, principally, in the imports they enable it to purchase. What may be called secondary benefits arise when the structure of comparative costs in two trading nations makes it mutually advantageous for each to specialize in a particular line of production (see Unit 9). Both can allocate resources more efficiently if they take advantage of *comparatively* low factor costs. They will, very probably, derive further efficiencies by producing for an extended market because this usually promotes a more extended division of labour and greater use of machinery per worker.

Let us discount the secondary benefits for a moment, and concentrate on the direct benefits: imports. Ostensibly, Britain seems to have benefited handsomely: retained imports were more than a quarter of GNP during the late nineteenth century, and four-fifths of a vital staple, wheat, came from abroad. But the obvious is not always a good guide in economic analysis. Substitutes could have been found for the imports, albeit at a higher cost. An economic historian would now typically address the problem by counterfactual reasoning: what would have been the extra cost, as a proportion of GNP, in producing at home the alternatives to acquiring imports by trade? Two scholars applying this line of reasoning have calculated that, in a self-sufficient economy, the extra cost of producing substitutes for all the imports into later nineteenth-century Britain would have been about 6 per cent of national income (Harley and McCloskey, 1981, pp.54–5). How do they reach such a comparatively modest figure when over a quarter of national income was actually being spent on imports? By postulating changes in the relative prices of such goods as cloth (now all home-consumed) and food (now all home grown). Because food would be relatively more expensive, consumption would shift to cheaper substitutes (less wheat more potatoes, for example.) The argument is logical, but does not enquire into the possible 'welfare' losses that would have followed from self-sufficiency. Would people have been better dressed, but less well fed? The important point for us is that commonplace statements about Britain 'depending' on international trade are implicitly quantitative, and the virtue of Harley and McCloskey's exercise is that it indicates a way we can answer the question 'By how much?'.

When international trade is analysed within a European-wide perspective, its 'gains' are, frankly, impossible to calculate by the method I have outlined. The 'gains' and 'losses' we impute to trade will turn upon its function in promoting or retarding economic development, particularly of modern industry. One school of thought, stretching from Frederick List to modern theorists of 'underdevelopment', argues that free trade between industrialized economies and primary producers accentuates the latters' relative economic backwardness. List, you will recall, made this an argument for import-substituting industrialization behind tariff walls. Does nineteenth-century Europe's economic history bear out the Listian view? Professor Pollard (whose views are rehearsed in Unit 9) has argued to the contrary: trade was a 'major channel of transmission of the process of industrialization' (Pollard, 1981, p.184). He puts forward a multilateral and dynamic trade model in which goods with a *high modern technology content* (including, say, steam-wound coal) exchange for goods with little or no such content. In this model, intermediary producers exploit their advantages (skilled labour and lower wages) as importers of semi-manufactures and machinery from a more technologically advanced country, and as exporters of finished goods to more backward economies. The trading pattern which exemplifies the model most clearly was the export of British cotton yarns, pig iron and coal (in whose production Britain had an overwhelming advantage) to France, Belgium and the Rhineland where skilled labour was abundant and wages lower. Producers in these regions in turn sold finished goods (such as cloth woven from British yarn) to markets in central and eastern Europe from which Britain imported grain and raw materials. The model is dynamic because we can understand how the intermediary position of producers having an 'uphill' trade with a more technologically advanced, higher-waged economy, but a 'downhill' one with more backward countries will shift over time. The import of capital goods will raise the technology content of their own exports and the relative advantage of cheap labour in finishing industries will pass to producers in the backward economies. Though highly simplified, the model is a fairly good 'fit' for the trade-driven diffusion of industrialization to Bohemia, Northern Italy and – in recent decades – such 'latecomers' as Portugal.

European foreign investment, c.1860–1914

In this section, we will analyse the timing, location and economic purpose of European capital exports, and investigate the connections between international finance and European international diplomacy. I will consider only long-term foreign investments, conventionally defined as those made for a year or more.

In our analysis, we must distinguish between the cumulative total of foreign investments, the aggregate total, and the flows of capital during any fixed period. The cumulative total (as in Table 11, p.142) gives a picture of the growth of property-ownership abroad. It is a 'net' sum made up of the annual flows of capital abroad, less capital repatriated when foreign investors sell their holdings to local businessmen. (North Americans, in particular, were buying back their stock from European investors by the late nineteenth century.) The aggregate total is a record of all purchases of foreign securities, and Figure 13 (p.144) shows a breakdown of the British aggregate over a fifty-year period.

Whatever indices we take, one thing is clear: the early twentieth century was a time when a high proportion of the world's capital stock was located outside the national boundaries of the rentier capitalists who owned that stock. In 1913, the cumulative total of foreign investment represented approximately 110 per cent of the combined GNP of the capital-exporting countries; around 1960–70, the comparable figure was no more than 12 per cent. The annual capital flows in 1913 were equal to about 5 per cent of the total GNP of the capital exporting nations; in 1960–70, they were equivalent to less than 1 per cent (Bairoch, 1976, p.100). It was capitalism, rather than socialism, that was 'international'.

Though we are concerned with capital exports after c.1860, it is worth saying something about the early nineteenth century just to establish why this date marked a turning point. Before 1800, Amsterdam had been Europe's largest money market and most significant source of foreign borrowing; as late as 1825, Dutch total foreign investments were still equal to

Britain's. These two commercial powers accounted for something like two-thirds of world capital exports. From this point, while Dutch capital exports stagnated, Britain's expanded, but so too did France's *at an even faster rate.* By the mid-1850s, the cumulative total of French foreign investments was almost five-sixths of British. This near equality of the two states' total foreign investments contrasts with the great preponderance of Britain's money market during the later nineteenth and early twentieth century.

Several factors differentiate the pre- and post-1860 situations: a rapid rate of British domestic capital formation in the earlier phase meant foreign borrowers faced strong competition for funds, while the demand for investment capital in newly settled regions of the world was as yet running at modest levels. Furthermore, though striking differences were to emerge in the locations of British and French investment, and the types of securities preferred, these were not much evident before 1860. European governments (Spain, Portugal, Greece) and governments on the European periphery (the Ottoman Empire, Egypt) were the chief customers for the foreign investment funds of Britain and France. Some British funds were invested in the enterprises in the Rhineland and Belgium, but the majority of issues were not of this type. As late as 1870, about three-fifths of British investments abroad were in government bonds, and much had gone into military rather than economic enterprises. Representative of these 'public', 'non-economic' foreign investments were the seventeen Ottoman state loans floated on the City and the Bourse between 1854 and 1877, and subscribed to by British and French in roughly equal proportions.

The 1860 watershed is not fixed term, and it was pre-dated by a political decision of some consequence for the pattern of British overseas investment and trade: this was the guaranteed rate of return offered by the government of British India to subscribers in Indian railway shares as part of a conscious policy of developing the sub-continent as a supplier of industrial raw materials and a market for British goods. India was not short of native capital, but her merchants and bakers normally expected a higher rate of return than the 4.97 per cent offered on railway equity. On the other hand, this was about 0.6 per cent above the average return on British railways, and as long as the Raj stood the investor could not lose. About 13 per cent of Indian government current revenue was being sent to Britain in the early twentieth century to pay railway dividends.

Table 11: Cumulative value of gross foreign investments (in millions of current $)

	1840	1870	1885	1900	1913
UK	720	3,850	7,850	12,500	20,300
France	300	2,500	3,300	5,200	9,000
Germany	-	-	2,000	3,600	4,700
Netherlands	200	500	1,000	1,100	1,200
Total Europe	1,600	8,800	16,500	26,000	40,000
USA	-	100	400	700	3,500
World Total	1,600	9,000	17,000	28,000	44,000

Source: Bairoch, 1976, p.101.

Table 12: Location of foreign investment c. 1913 as % of total foreign investment for the major capital exporters

Location	Investing country			
	UK	France	Germany	Europe
Europe	5.2	51.9	44.0	26.8
N America	35.2	5.5	19.8	24.3
S America	18.5	17.7	15.5	17.3
Africa	12.3	9.9	8.6	9.7
Asia	17.8	13.8	12.1	16.4
Oceania	11.0	1.1	–	5.5
Total	100	100	100	100

Source: Bairoch, 1976, p.104.

Exercise   I want you now to turn to the information conveyed in Tables 11 and 12 and summarize the major trends they indicate, and any differences in the location of British and other European investment in 1913. Do you see any parallels with the geography of trade?

Discussion   The figures bring home the huge growth in the world volume of overseas investment, during the 45 years before the First World War, and the fact that Europe was, effectively, 'the World's Banker', with Britain very much the dominant partner. In 1913, more than half of European foreign investment was owned by UK subjects. Given that the price level of capital goods was probably 30 per cent *lower* in 1913 than in 1840, the 'real' growth in foreign investment was that much higher. Table 12 reveals striking differences in the locational pattern of British and other European capital holding: by 1913, British overseas investment was concentrated in the Americas, and Europe was no longer important (though it had been in 1870). For French and German investors, however, Europe was still much the most important site of investment, though by 1913 they were beginning to follow their British counterparts in looking for investment opportunities overseas. In Britain's case, there was a fair correspondence between the geography of investment and of trade, and this is not surprising since much British investment was trade-related. In the case of France, the next largest investor, the correspondence was much weaker – if it existed at all. Russia was the most important recipient of French investment – accounting for at least a quarter of total French foreign holdings – but provided France with only 5 per cent of her imports and absorbed only 1 per cent of French exports. While Switzerland, Belgium, Italy and the Netherlands together absorbed over a quarter of France's exports, they received only 6 per cent of French foreign investments.

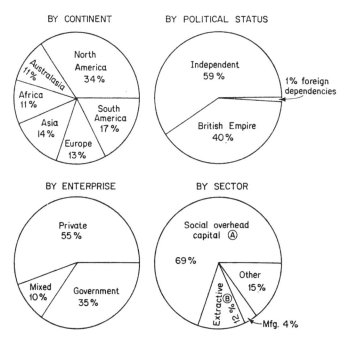

BY CONTINENT

BY POLITICAL STATUS

BY ENTERPRISE

BY SECTOR

Figure 13
Export of capital from
Britain. (From M.Simon,
'The pattern of new British
portfolio investment, 1865–
1914', in Capital
Movements and Economic
Development: Proceedings
of a conference held by the
International Economic
Association, *Macmillan,*
1967.)

Ⓐ Includes transportation, public utilities and public works

Ⓑ Includes agriculture and mining

The segmented circle diagrams reproduced in Figure 13 are the bare bones of the pioneer application of the computer to historical research. Back in the 1960s, over 41,000 separate foreign and colonial share transactions recorded in the British financial press between 1865 and 1914 were placed on a data base. This allowed for classification by continent and country, climatic and ethnic region, the political status of the recipient nation (whether independent state, British Dominion or dependent colony), the type of issuer (whether public limited company or state/local government or some 'mixed' enterprise), the industry from which the security was issued (whether transport or extractive or manufacturing), and the type of security issued.

Exerrcise   Use the segmented circles (in Figure 13), summarizing the British experience of overseas investment between 1865 and 1914, and say whether these statements are true, false or not verifiable by the data:

1   The British Empire was always the most favoured field of British foreign investment.

2   Most investment went to tropical countries where it enjoyed a far higher rate of return than in Britain.

3   Europe never accounted for more than 13 per cent of British foreign investment.

4   Regions of European settlement attracted a disproportionate share of British investment.

5   British investors preferred to invest in private rather than public enterprise, and were most attracted to railway share capital.

6   There was a long-term trend away from investment in government securities towards investment in private enterprise.

Specimen Answers   1   False, independent states attracted a larger share.

2   Two statements in one here; the first part is false. Even if a significant element of South American investment was in the tropics, the preponderance of temperate regions is clear. The second part is not verifiable; the data before you give no information on rates of return.

3   False. If Europe attracted only 5.2 per cent of British investment around 1913 (Table 11), yet attracted 13 per cent of aggregate investment over the whole fifty-year period, then at some time it must have attracted quite a bit more than 13 per cent.

4   True.

5   Two statements again. The first is true, and the second highly likely. You would be right to assume that railways constituted the largest share of 'social overhead capital'.

6   True. If you said 'not verifiable' you have not been paying attention, because earlier you were told that in 1870 three-fifths of British overseas investment was in government bonds. Over the whole period, the proportion was significantly smaller. The trend must have been away from investment of this character.

There are some key points we must add to this overall picture of British foreign investment before attempting a comparison with French. First, a common characteristic of all foreign investment (British or otherwise) in this period was that around 90 per cent would now be classified as 'portfolio' rather than 'direct'. (A 'portfolio' holding is one accounting for less than 30 per cent of the share equity in a private enterprise, 'direct' more than 30 per cent.) This was due to the concentration of foreign investment in social overhead capital, above all railways, which is typically 'lumpy'. A lot must be invested in a railway before it will provide a service or return a profit. Only governments or big joint-stock companies (or 'mixed' enterprises) can act as entrepreneurs in this sector, and only by attracting large numbers of small investors can the risks be safely spread. In the rare instances when British investors did own and control foreign enterprises (the Calcutta jutes mills are an example) ownership was usually dispersed amongst many share-holders for much the same reason. Few large British businesses directly invested abroad, and were not to do so until it became more attractive to invest in manufacturing.

Secondly, the small proportion invested in manufacturing abroad before 1914 suggests that neither the flow nor location of British investments was much affected by protective tariffs. Had manufacturers felt excluded from foreign markets by tariff barriers they would have 'jumped over' them by buying plant and producing on the spot. (This was one reason for French, German and Belgian direct investment in Central and Eastern Europe which was a larger – though still small – proportion of total foreign investment by these countries.) But as Britain's largest export market – India – did not have the political power to implement protection, while tariff levels in other non-European markets were low, there was little incentive for direct inward investment.

Thirdly, the export of capital from Britain shows a close symmetry with the export of labour, and this fact will explain much of the difference between Britain and France as capital exporting countries. Until the early twentieth century, the annual flow of migrants from the UK made by far the largest contribution to total European overseas migration; only between 1901 and 1910 was British migration (with which Irish migration was then classified) exceeded by Italian. British and Irish migrants were attracted principally to North America, and upsurges of migration were accompanied by surges in capital exports. The North American and British economic cycles of boom and slump were closely, but inversely related: when employment and output grew rapidly in North America, they grew slowly in Britain, and vice versa. North American demand for investment capital and labour tended to be greatest when there was little demand for new investment in Britain and unemployment, particularly in construction and agriculture, was high. There was 'an intercontinental rivalry for resources' (Thomas, 1968, p.47). No other European power participated in this rivalry in quite the same way. The poor, southern European states (Italy, Portugal) had abundant labour but no surplus capital (in fact, they imported more capital remitted by migrants abroad than they exported). France had surplus capital, but a chronic labour shortage. Up to the late 1880s, there were significant numbers of inter-continental migrants from Germany, but even when they reached an annual maximum of 134,000 in that decade this was less than a third of the flow from the UK (326,000 per year during the 1880s). Overseas migration from Germany fell to a trickle after 1890 because industrialization and urbanization created massive labour demands. In the four years before the outbreak of war, only 16,000 overseas migrants left Germany annually, compared with 358,000 leaving the UK. In an industrializing and urbanizing economy, labour cannot be employed without capital; as we have already seen (Unit 9) the rate of domestic investment – as a proportion of GNP – was much higher in late nineteenth-century Germany. It was a state whose economic resources were concentrated in the national territory. Britain's were dispersed around the globe: over the 50-year period, less than a third of the capital 'called up' on the City was actually invested in the domestic economy.

Lastly, detailed analysis of Simon's data (and subsequent research by Davis and Huttenback, 1988) refutes the well-known thesis that capital exports were causally related to the acquisition of dependent colonies during the 'New Imperialism'. Although the British Empire consistently attracted two-fifths of British overseas investment, most went to 'white' Dominions which were acquiring real autonomy in economic affairs. (Canada, for example, initiated industrialization behind a tariff barrier which gave no preference to British goods.) The 'political cover' of the imperial connection was not what attracted British investors, but the market opportunities afforded by rapid economic development in regions of European settlement during the late nineteenth and early twentieth century. If we analyse European overseas investment in per capita terms, then the degree to which it favoured culturally familiar communities in the wider world is overwhelming: investments in countries of European settlement amounted to about 131 dollars per habitant in 1913, while in other countries the comparable figure was about 11 dollars. On a per capita basis, the countries with the highest level of European investment in 1913 were Canada, Argentina, Australia, New Zealand and South Africa.

That said, '*finance imperialism*' is not so much a myth as a matter of looking in the wrong place at the wrong time. For if we focus, not on the powers which exported capital, but on the peripheral, underdeveloped societies which received it, then it is clear that state indebtedness to foreign bondholders was part of a process by which their sovereignty was infringed and/or violated. The Ottoman loans, for example, led to a private Franco-British bank – the Imperial Ottoman, founded in 1853 – acting as Turkey's state bank and the executive of the Turkish treasury, with the sole right to issue paper money. When the state was finally bankrupted in 1875, the national debt was placed under international administration, and a quarter of public revenues were directly collected by a foreign agency to service debt charges. The Egyptian government raised eight foreign loans, mainly through French banks, between 1862 and 1873. Foreign indebtedness, and the influx of a parasitic class of bondholders' agents who demanded extra-territorial legal status, fatally corrupted native authority structures. When the state went bankrupt, its national debt was also placed under international administration. After a nationalist uprising against foreign influence, Britain occupied Egypt in 1882. A similar sequence had led to the French occupation of Tunisia in 1881. Other examples, albeit less clear cut, could be found in Morocco and Persia. From the perspective of the underdeveloped, traditional state the pattern of events does fit into a general model of 'finance imperialism', though not one which identifies imperialism with 'monopoly capitalism', for no European economy had evinced much tendency to monopoly before the mid-1880s.

Finance and diplomacy: French foreign investments

In 1913, France, not Britain, was Europe's banker, and the largest investor in Europe's Muslim flank. The value of French foreign investments in Europe was more than four times greater than British. French subscribers accounted for about three-fifths of Ottoman and a half of Egyptian state loans, while over half the foreign private capital in Egypt was French-owned. This is somewhat surprising, given that Britain had been the occupying power in Egypt since 1882, but the Eastern Mediterranean was a region of considerable commercial and cultural importance for France. French capital and engineering expertise, with Egyptian corvée labour, built the Suez canal. Tense relations with Britain between 1882 and the *Entente cordiale* of 1904 are to be explained largely by France's resentment at exclusion from a country felt to be rightly 'hers'.

Loans to governments were well over half the total of French foreign investments in 1913 (compare this with the British proportion). Public securities almost invariably bore a fixed interest, but one lower than the return on riskier private equity, so the preference for government bonds demonstrated the caution of the French small saver. Most public investments mobilized on behalf of Russia, Turkey or the new Balkan states had an economic purpose, but – as we would expect – economic interests were more closely intertwined with political power in these transactions than was the case with purely private financing.

Exercise   Where was the relationship between French finance and French diplomacy exceptionally close and strategically vital?

Discussion   In Russia, where nearly half the national debt was owned by foreigners in 1914, and four-fifths of the foreign holdings were in French names. The French share of private foreign investment in Russia was much smaller: about a third, compared with slightly less than a quarter owned by British and one-fifth by German investors.

France and Russia had entered a military alliance in 1892, and financial diplomacy both preceded this agreement, as well as helping cement it. Until the late 1880s, Germans were the major investors in Russian funds, and the reversal in European diplomacy which brought France and Russia together was precipitated by Bismarck's closure of Germany's money markets to the Tsarist authorities at a time of deteriorating relations amongst the three eastern empires. French financial institutions, with the consent and increasingly the support of the French government, arranged for the floating of a large Russian loan on the Bourse. After the Dual Alliance was sealed, the French government and the institutions co-operated in ensuring as wide a sale as possible to the investing public. By 1913, a total of 1.6 million French people had overcome their republican scruples to invest in Tsarist Russia, which they saw as guaranteeing the security of the nation and holding out the best promise for the recovery of Alsace-Lorraine – as well as a profitable haven for savings. 'No capital movement was more important in shaping the destinies of [Europe]' (Feis, 1930, p.212).

During the run-up to the First World War, finance became an overt arm of French diplomacy in Eastern Europe and the Balkans. New Russian flotations in France were only permitted in 1913 after Russia agreed to augment its army and build certain strategic railways. Following the Turkish revolution of 1908, the constitutional, nationalist government attempted to by-pass the services of the foreign-owned Ottoman Bank, but the refusal of the London and Berlin money markets to support its foreign borrowing obliged Turkey to resort once again to Paris. As part of the financial arrangements agreed with the Bourse, the French foreign office extracted orders for the French armaments firm, Schneider. Under the Franco-Ottoman accord of April 1914, France obtained considerable economic advantages for its companies operating in the Ottoman Empire, cultural advantages for French schools in the Levant, and political advantages in the recognition by the Ottoman government of French zones of influence within the empire.

While French capital exports within Europe acquired this political complexion during the pre-war years, in other continents they were, like Britain's, strictly market-oriented. Between 1900 and 1913, the proportion of extra-European investments in the French total rose substantially, and those going to Latin America and the French colonies increased threefold.

Conclusion

What conclusions can we draw from this analysis of the growth of European international trade and investment? Provocatively, I would suggest that by 1914 the 'economy' had 'outgrown' the state. In the course of the previous fifty years, capitalist enterprise had 'spilled over' the confines of the national state and, by making global connections, created an international system that was by 1913 determining economic development within its constituent national parts. In other words, the phenomenon which we now refer to as economic 'globalization' was already in train by eve of the First World War. The breakdown in the European balance, the inter-war collapse of global trade and the European 'Thirty Years War' of 1914–45, were a long parenthesis in international economic history radically different from what had gone before and what came subsequently. The trends towards international economic integration, discussed in this unit, have been felt with fuller force since the formation of the European Economic Community in 1957, and the liberalization of world capital markets since the 1960s. Though fundamental changes in economic organization separate us from the early twentieth century, there is also a great deal that is 'familiar' – even though we might sense a certain reversal in fortune. Foreign investment is now seen as a key to *our* economic well-being, and international money movements are now so untrammelled as to nullify the economic policies and objectives of national governments. For better or worse we are heirs to the late nineteenth- and early twentieth-century world economy created by European economic endeavour.

References

Bairoch, P. (1975), *The Economic Development of the Third World since 1900*, Methuen, London.

Bairoch, P. (1976), *Commerce extérieur et développement économique de l'Europe au XIXe siècle*, Mouton.

Bairoch, P. (1989), 'European Trade Policy, 1815–1914' in P. Mathias and S. Pollard, (eds), *The Cambridge Economic History of Europe*, vol.VIII *The Industrial Economies: The Development of Economic and Social Policies*, Cambridge University Press, Cambridge.

Davis, L. and Huttenback, R. (1988), *Mammon and the Pursuit of Empire: the Economics of British Imperialism*, Cambridge University Press, Cambridge.

Edelstein, M. (1981), 'Foreign investment and empire 1860–1914', in R. Floud and D. McCloskey (eds), *The Economic History of Britain since 1700*, vol.2, Cambridge University Press, Cambridge.

Feis, H. (1930), *Europe: the World's Banker, 1870–1914*, Yale University Press, New Haven.

Hall, A.R. (ed.) (1968), *The Export of Capital from Britain, 1870–1914*, Methuen, London.

Hanson, J.R. (1980), *Trade in Transition: Exports from the Third World, 1840–1900*, Academic Press, New York.

Harley, C.K. and McCloskey, D. (1981), 'Foreign trade: competition and the expanding international economy', in R. Floud and D. McCloskey (eds), *The Economic History of Britain since 1700*, vol.2, Cambridge University Press, Cambridge.

Imlah, A.H. (1958), *Economic Elements in the Pax Britannica*, Havard University Press, Boston, Mass.

Mitchell, B.R. and Deane, P. (1962), *Abstract of British Historical Statistics*, Cambridge University Press, Cambridge.

Pollard, S. (1981), *Peaceful Conquest: the Industrialization of Europe 1760–1970*, Oxford University Press, Oxford.

Simon, M. (1968), 'The Pattern of New British Portfolio Foreign Investment, 1865–1914', in A.R. Hall (ed.).

Thomas, B. (1968), 'Migration and International Investment', in A.R. Hall (ed.).

Index